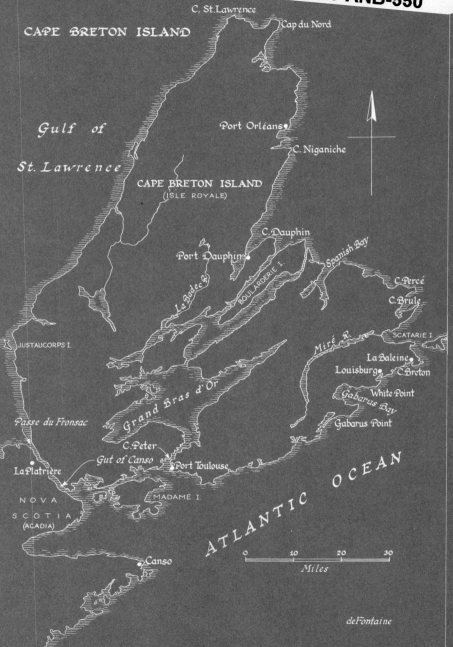

C. St.Lawrence

Cap du Nord

CAPE BRETON ISLAND

Port Orléans

C. Niganiche

Gulf of

St. Lawrence

CAPE BRETON ISLAND
(ISLE ROYALE)

C. Dauphin

Port Dauphin

Spanish Bay

La Badec R.

BOULARDERIE I.

C.Percé

C.Brule

Miré R.

SCATARIE I.

JUSTAUCORPS I.

La Baleine

Louisburg

C.Breton

White Point

Gabarus Bay

Grand Bras d'Or

Gabarus Point

Passe du Fronsac

C.Peter

Gut of Canso

Port Toulouse

La Platrière

N O V A

S C O T I A
(ACADIA)

MADAME I.

A T L A N T I C   O C E A N

Canso

0   10   20   30

Miles

deFontaine

THE FANTASTIC BREED

Books by Leon Phillips

THE FANTASTIC BREED: AMERICANS IN KING GEORGE'S WAR

SPLIT BAMBOO

QUEEN'S BLADE

WHEN THE WIND BLOWS

THE FANTASTIC BREED

Americans in King George's War

Leon Phillips

Doubleday & Company, Inc.
Garden City, New York

Library of Congress Catalog Card Number 68–10599
Copyright © 1968 by Doubleday & Company, Inc.
All Rights Reserved
Printed in the United States of America
First Edition

For
Margot

THE FANTASTIC BREED

1

Rains were heavy in the spring of 1742, the sun was warm, and settlers on the Massachusetts Bay frontier expected bumper crops. Corn was growing tall on the rolling hills, wheat and rye and oats were sturdy, and the vines in vegetable gardens were already heavy with ascutasquash. In the forests, deer and other game were plentiful, wild fowl settled in large numbers on the lakes, and the Connecticut River was teeming with shad. No one in the wilderness towns would go hungry.

Trappers laden with bales of beaver and fox pelts rested for a night or two behind the high, protective palisades of Springfield, the area's principal fortress town, and boasted of the prices Boston merchants would pay for their wares. Traders from Lynn and Braintree and other seaboard towns rode their pack mules through the deep woods carrying iron skillets, axes, and seeds newly arrived from England to the farthest reaches of the colony.

On April 1, Governor William Shirley concluded his triumphant annual report to King George II with a bold prediction: "This will be the most prosperous year in more than one hundred years of Massachusetts Bay's history!"

Shirley's optimism was shared by the residents of Bartonsfield, a village above Springfield on the Connecticut, a few miles north of the place where the Chicopee flowed into the great river. Abel Cooper, who owned the general store, had cash in his purse for the first time since he had moved west to the frontier six years earlier. Edward Green, his brother-in-law, spoke of enlarging his inn, the only public house in the district other than the two in Springfield. And Thomas Purdy, the horse dealer, planned to go off to Boston with his sons on a buying trip as soon as the trails and roads became dry.

Isaiah Collins and his entire family, seven sons and four daughters, cleared an additional one hundred and fifty acres on the heights above Bartonsfield, the older boys felling trees and digging out stumps, the girls burning brush. Martha Collins wanted to help, too, but she was expecting another baby, and so confined herself to cooking and to cleaning the family's five-room log house.

Thaddeus Barton, whose father had been the first to settle in the area, sent an enthusiastic letter describing the village's prosperity to his friend, William Pepperrell, one of the colony's most prominent landowners and commander of the inactive Massachusetts Bay militia. "Our plantations," Barton declared, "soon will rival those of the east in size and affluence. The future is ours."

And, indeed, so it seemed.

Then, on the night of April 23, about two hours after sundown, Bartonsfield was destroyed by a large band of Indians in green and yellow war paint. No one ever knew how many raiders took part in the attack. A commission of three men sent north from Springfield to investigate the tragedy estimated there had been at least seventy-five warriors in the party, but Captain Samuel Scales, the head of the group, admitted he was guessing.

The braves struck at several places simultaneously, and it was evident that the assault had been planned with great care. Abel Cooper and his wife were murdered and scalped in their bed. Their store was looted so thoroughly that nothing was left except a few kegs of salt, two bolts of cloth, and some wooden dolls that Cooper had been whittling in his spare time for the children of the neighborhood.

Edward Green's inn was burned to the ground, and the

mutilated body of the proprietor was found in the gutted ruins, as were those of his son and two nephews. Every horse in Thomas Purdy's stables was stolen, and he died trying to defend himself. His elder son was captured by the warriors and tortured to death, but the younger managed to escape on foot and concealed himself in the forest until the raiders had gone. The enemy column passed within a few feet of his hiding place, and he told Captain Scales he had heard two men speaking French, a language with which he was familiar because he had paid several visits to the villages of French Huguenot refugees from religious persecution on the Massachusetts Bay frontier.

Isaiah Collins and all twelve members of his family tried valiantly to fight off the intruders, but were overpowered. Not one survived. The three youngest Collins children, two girls and a boy, died of pistol wounds in the head, and since the available evidence indicated that the Indians carried only muskets and bows, Captain Scales, in his report to the Governor, expressed the opinion that Collins had killed them himself rather than let them fall into the hands of the enemy.

Thaddeus Barton, his wife and their three small children were more fortunate. They hid in a cramped root cellar beneath their house, pulling a stone trap door shut above their heads. They spent the entire night in the dark, almost suffocating, and when they emerged the following morning they found that their house had been burned over their heads, and that only the gutted, still-smoking skeleton remained.

The attack on Bartonsfield electrified the entire frontier, from the Maine District of Massachusetts Bay to Pennsylvania. The immediate problem was that of determining the identity of the warriors who had made the attack, and the question was difficult. Relations between the British colonists in Massachusetts Bay and the nations of the powerful Iroquois Confederation had been excellent for more than a decade, and two scouts sent by Captain Scales to the main towns of the Mohawk and Seneca returned from New York swearing that these neighboring tribes were not guilty.

Colonel Samuel Waldo of the Maine District paid a personal visit to the sachem, or chief, of the Algonkin tribe, and subsequently sent a letter by special courier to Governor Shirley, saying that no Algonkin braves had gone on the warpath. He indicated, however, that the Algonkin had been approached in recent months by agents from Quebec who had offered them muskets, whisky, and considerable quantities of French gold if they would attack the English settlements to their south.

Although the word of Indians was always considered open to question, the Algonkin chief's story seemed authentic. The frontiersmen quickly recalled that Billy Purdy had declared he had heard two members of the war party speaking French. And someone who had visited Quebec on a trading mission informed Governor Shirley that the Micmac of Newfoundland smeared themselves with green and yellow paint when they went on the warpath.

Colonel Pepperrell immediately challenged the latter claim, but himself presented another. The most powerful of the savage nations in French Canada, the Abnaki, he wrote the Governor, did use green and yellow paint when they went to war. He was convinced, he said, that the assault had been made by braves either prodded or inspired by the French.

While the frontier dwellers digested this warning, which was relayed to them by officers of the quickly activated colonial militia, the enemy struck again. Their initial success had made them bold, and they sent a column of more than two hundred warriors to Springfield.

The principal wilderness fort of Massachusetts Bay was

ready for any intruder. Virtually every man and every boy of sixteen or over was enlisted in Captain Scales' militia company, and approximately one hundred and fifty defenders were on duty when, on the night of May 11, the raiders attacked. Marksmen armed with the long frontier rifles that, in the hands of experts, were the deadliest weapons in all of North America, were stationed on platforms behind the high palisades of upright pine logs. Eight small cannon emplaced in the blockhouses, directly behind the walls, formed the hard core of Springfield's defenses.

Even more important was the caliber of the men who were responsible for guarding the frontier. Scales and his five subordinate officers had spent their entire lives in the wilderness, were familiar with all the techniques of Indian fighting, and understood the savages. The sergeants and corporals had enjoyed long experience in dealing with the Indians, too. Many earned their living in civilian life as trappers, hunters, and traders, and they remained calm as they watched stealthy figures creeping toward the palisades across the open fields outside the town.

Members of the company went quietly from house to house, informing the inhabitants of Springfield that a battle would begin at any moment. Small children were allowed to sleep undisturbed, while the women and older girls filled buckets with water from their wells and waited silently in their darkened kitchens for the assault to begin. The self-discipline of the community was extraordinary. There was no hysteria, no panic. Everyone understood the need for quiet.

The attackers, advancing in a ragged line, halted about fifty feet from the walls and sent a shower of flaming arrows above the palisades into the town. Thanks to the vigilance of Springfield's housewives and their daughters, the flames were extinguished as rapidly as the arrows fell. Then, as the Indians notched fresh arrows in their bows, a signal was passed down the ramparts.

The deep quiet of the frontier was broken as one hundred and fifty long rifles spoke more or less simultaneously. The Indians, taken completely by surprise, retreated into a patch of woods, reformed their ranks, and charged furiously, hoping to storm the palisades with ladders made of vines. Again a volley was fired, and again they were driven back.

By this time, Scales and two of his lieutenants, directing the defense from one of the towers, had located the enemy reserve force in the woods. The time had come to use the cannon, and five of the guns were trained on the spot. There were few experienced artillerymen on the frontier, and handling the six-pounder guns was an unfamiliar art. But the crews made up in zeal what they lacked in skill, and sent a fusillade of iron balls crashing through the oak and beech and pine.

No one ever knew whether the fire was more effective than the defenders had dared to hope, or whether the booming of the cannon and the sound of shot smashing through foliage had frightened savages unaccustomed to an artillery barrage. Whatever the reason, the Indians lost heart and fled. The warriors who made up the assault force realized their comrades were deserting them, and they, too, retreated.

War canoes had been hidden in the brush along the banks of the Connecticut River, and the militia officers in the watchtowers caught a final glimpse of the enemy as they paddled upstream, vanishing into the night. The raid had been a total failure, and in their panicky flight the Indians had broken an inviolable custom of all North American tribes: They had left their dead behind.

In all, thirty-one bodies were found. Twenty-eight of the dead were braves dressed in buckskin trousers and moccasins, their torsos and faces streaked with greasy green and yellow paint, their long scalp locks matted. They were far shorter than the warriors of the Iroquois nations, and somewhat darker than the Algonkin. Captain Scales assumed they were Abnaki.

Of far greater interest to the militia officers were the bodies of the remaining three raiders. One, who wore boots, breeches of stout wool, and a lawn shirt, had light brown hair and a fair skin. Papers he carried in a pouch at his belt positively identified him as Lieutenant Henri de Maribaux, personal assistant to the Military Intendant of Quebec. His presence with the raiders was indisputable proof that the attack had been encouraged, and probably directed, by the official leaders of New France.

The other bodies were those of half-breeds, and they, too, carried papers. One, it appeared, was familiar with the Maine District and had sold furs to Colonel Waldo, the leading citizen of that region. It was a reasonably good guess that the half-breeds had acted as the war party's guides.

The recovered documents were so valuable that Scales rode in person to Boston and presented them to Governor Shirley, who immediately called an emergency session of the Massachusetts Bay Assembly, or colonial legislature. The basic situation, Shirley explained, was simple—and shocking.

A few months earlier, Great Britain and France had gone to war with one another in a conflict that involved most of Europe's great powers. Now that war had spread to British and French possessions in the New World. And the presence of Lieutenant de Maribaux with the Springfield raiders proved beyond all reasonable doubt that the French had committed the crime, unpardonable in the eyes of English colonists, of initiating Indian attacks against the wilderness settlements.

William Vaughan, a graduate of Harvard College whose fishing fleet had earned him a fortune at his home in the Maine District and who was known as the "Codfish King," expressed the sentiments of the Assembly after listening to Governor Shirley's address. "When innocent women and children can no longer dwell in safety on the frontier," he told the hushed legislators, "only one course of action is open to honorable men. New France has issued a challenge. We must accept it, no matter what the cost. This means war—to the death!"

But although the colonies continued to be harassed by Indian raids, full-scale war did not come to the New World for many months. Great Britain, engaged in a war of her own on the continent of Europe, could not provide adequate defenses for the English colonies, and they were forced to protect themselves. Massachusetts Bay was the first colony to prepare actively for the struggle that came to be known in the New World as King George's War. The Assembly granted Governor Shirley the authority to raise six regiments of militia, four in Massachusetts Bay proper and two in the Maine District, and taxes were imposed on all property owners in the colony for the purpose. Later, William Pepperrell was given the temporary rank of Major General and was named commander of the force, and Samuel Waldo was promoted to Brigadier General, in charge of the Maine District contingent.

Neighboring colonies soon followed suit and began calling up militia regiments of their own. By the fall of frontier, and once again wilderness settlers could sleep in 1742, troops armed with long rifles patrolled the entire relative peace.

"The measures taken by Massachusetts Bay and her sister colonies may prevent catastrophes similar to the destruction of Bartonsfield," the energetic Governor Shirley wrote to the Colonial Office in London. "Nevertheless, I lack confidence in the efforts we have made. The frontier is long, and the opportunities afforded the enemy to create mischief are innumerable."

Codfish King William Vaughan, who had accepted a commission as Colonel of a regiment from the Maine District, put the matter more bluntly. "We lack the men to defend our whole wilderness," he wrote General Pepperrell. "There is only one adequate defense. We must attack New France!"

Pepperrell was inclined to agree, but a number of political problems dampened the prospects of mounting such an attack. Everywhere, troops had been mustered only for service within the borders of each colony, and the governors shared the reluctance of the legislatures to send troops on a foreign expedition. Also, there were squabbles between military leaders. Massachusetts Bay assumed that her generals would command a joint force, but Connecticut, New York, and Pennsylvania violently disagreed, each insisting that her own senior commanders were the best soldiers in the New World.

Meanwhile, the French made their own preparations for war on a vast scale. More willing than the British to gamble, the ministers of King Louis XV sent several regiments of Regulars across the Atlantic to bolster the mighty fortress of Louisburg, on Cape Breton Island, which guarded the entrance to the St. Lawrence River. Millions of francs were spent to strengthen Louisburg, already the most powerful fort in all of North and South America. Agents fanned out from this great bastion to arouse the Micmac, the Abnaki, and the Algonkin, and a fleet of warships flying the gold-and-white lily banner of France took shelter in the shadow of Louisburg's formidable cannon.

Blood would be shed again and again in the English colonies, and her people would endure great suffering before necessity forced them to band together in an enterprise unprecedented in the history of New World warfare.

The War of the Austrian Succession, sometimes known as the Seven Years' War, was a struggle in which, at one time or another, every major European power and many of the smaller nations of the continent took part. At its conclusion, William Pitt the elder, later to become the most renowned British statesman of the age, called it "the war nobody wanted."

Reasonable men everywhere agreed with Pitt's pamphlet, *The Senselessness of the Seven Years' War.* "All nations were reluctant to join in the fight," he wrote, "yet each was afraid to stand aside, fearful that its own interests would be injured. We call ourselves England or France or Prussia, as the case may be, but a nation is like an individual. Men band together when they are frightened; so, too, do nations. Men are greedy; so, too, are nations."

When Pitt spoke of greed, his readers knew at once that he referred to the young king of Prussia, a military and administrative genius of such talents that he was already being called Frederick the Great. In 1740, Frederick was the master of a heavily populated country, small in area, with a strong military tradition. Enlarging the army left to him by his father, Frederick had created a superbly trained force of one hundred thousand men.

Dynamically ambitious, he, and his subjects with him, wanted to expand the borders of Prussia. In a letter to his good friend, Voltaire, the playwright, historian, poet, and essayist who was the literary giant of the century, Frederick was remarkably candid. "I want the Silesian duchies that adjoin my land," he wrote. "It matters little that they belong to Austria. Her claim to them, in essence, is no more valid than mine. But my arms are stronger; therefore my will shall prevail."

Frederick chose a perfect time for his "Silesian adventure." A new ruler had just mounted the throne of Austria—the pretty, fair-skinned Grand Duchess Maria Theresa, who was little more than a girl. Not for several years would she become known as the Empress, and a still longer time would pass before she would be recognized as a wise, humane ruler.

Now, early in her accession, there was discontent everywhere in her realm. The Austrians themselves were unhappy at the prospect of being ruled by a woman. In Hungary, which was part of her domain, men spoke openly of establishing an independent nation. And in Bohemia, also part of her empire, there was a rising swell of discord. Administrators in Budapest and Prague wrote in alarm to Vienna that revolts were threatening, and Austrian troops were sent into both Hungary and Bohemia to pacify these areas.

Therefore, as Frederick well knew, only a few divisions of Austrians held Silesia. Late in November, 1740, his regiments began mustering in secret. There were units of magnificently trained heavy infantry, able to march for days at a time with little rest. There were contingents of light infantry, assault troops anxious to demonstrate their courage to the world. At night, when the dark roads were deserted, the cannon of the Prussian artillery rumbled down dusty back lanes, skirting towns and villages. The last to move were the squadrons of cavalry, audacious but disciplined.

Gradually, inching toward their goal, the Prussian divisions mobilized in the deep forests facing the Oder River. It was the custom, as in earlier and subsequent wars, for

a nation to issue a formal declaration before opening
hostilities. But Frederick ignored tradition. Suddenly, on
the night of December 16, the Prussian cannon opened fire
on the startled Austrians across the river. The Prussian
sappers, or engineers, lashed barges together and made
bridges of them. The cavalry rode into Silesia at full tilt,
closely followed by the assault infantry, with the stolid
heavy infantry behind them.

Badly outnumbered, the Austrians were forced to retreat, and only a few small, heavily fortified garrisons
held out against the enemy. The bulk of the Austrian
force fell back on the Bohemian border, and within a
few days, Frederick was in possession of all Silesia.

In 1741, Maria Theresa made a dramatic, personal
appeal to the Hungarians, begging them to join her.
According to one legend, never confirmed but almost impossible to disprove, she appeared before the nobles and
prominent commoners of Budapest with her infant son in
her arms, and cried, "Help save my throne for my baby!"

Her tactics were successful, and the Hungarians rallied
to her cause, as did the Bohemians and the Austrians
themselves. In a time of great danger, Maria Theresa's
subjects united behind her.

But Frederick was not to be denied; his legions
crushed the armies of the Austrians in battle after battle.

The rest of Europe awakened to an obvious fact: a new
major power, Prussia, had become a force of consequence
on the continent. King Louis XV of France, anxious to
obtain his share of grandeur—and conquest—sent a courier
to Frederick with the message, "France is your ally."

The race to join in the war had begun. Imperial Russia,
afraid she would be menaced by a Franco-Prussian alliance, came to the aid of Austria. Sweden, her traditional
enemy, joined the French and Prussians, as did the
Electorate of Bavaria and the Kingdom of Sardinia. Spain,
whose royal family was related to that of Austria, entered

the struggle for her own reasons: if Maria Theresa could be deposed, a Spanish member of the Hapsburg family would have a legitimate claim to the Austrian throne.

The circle grew still larger. Saxony, Frederick's neighbor, joined the Austrians for the sake of her own protection, fearing that she, too, might be overpowered by the land-hungry Prussians. The little Electorate of Hanover, which had given England her current ruling monarch, King George II—and before him his father, George I—came to the assistance of Austria for the same reasons. The Sardinians, feeling that they had chosen the wrong side, gave up their alliance with Frederick and came into the war a second time, on Austria's side.

The most important move was made by England and her firm ally, Holland. Their joint traditional enemy was France, and the entrance of Louis XV into the war as the comrade-in-arms of Frederick almost automatically placed the British and Dutch in opposition to Prussia. London and Amsterdam had successfully joined forces with Austria against the French earlier in the century, in what had been called the War of the Spanish Succession. In that struggle, they had defeated the armies of Louis XIV, which had been regarded as the most powerful on earth. What they had done in one war, they believed, they could do again.

Imperial Russia simplified matters by inflicting a series of stunning defeats on the Swedes. Both nations then retired from the war, and the northern front was quiet. Meanwhile, Austria won a number of significant victories in Italy and Bavaria, thus neutralizing her enemies in those sectors.

Frederick wisely decided the time had come to consolidate his gains and end the bloodshed, at least temporarily. He made his peace with Maria Theresa, a peace that would be broken and then patched up again many times before the war finally ended in 1748.

A unique situation now developed. With other participants only too relieved to drop out, the major powers left facing each other were Great Britain and France, neither of which had started the war, neither of which initially had any intention of joining it.

Great Britain had built the world's most powerful navy, and her warships controlled the high seas off the shores of Europe. But her margin of superiority was not as great as it was destined to become a little more than a half-century later. Her navy was stronger than that of France, but only slightly stronger. Many military experts considered the French army better than that of her enemy, but the edge was very slight. The British refused to concede that France could defeat them on land, and the French high command privately admitted that the two sides were evenly matched.

"On the surface," William Pitt later wrote, "it seemed absurd that two major powers should remain at odds, when they had no quarrel strong enough to impel them to go to war against one another in the first place."

"Neither the French nor the British," Voltaire observed, "could hope to win a clear-cut victory. Why, then, did they fight?"

Why? Common people on both sides asked the same question. In London, in Paris, and in the provinces of both countries, the war was unpopular. British newspapers freely criticized the ministers of George II for plunging the nation into a struggle that appeared to have no real purpose. In France, where censorship was strict, no one dared to criticize the Crown openly, but there were veiled hints of dissatisfaction in plays, poems, and popular songs of the day. It was difficult to whip up enthusiasm for the war on either side.

Nevertheless, there was indeed a motive that impelled the governments of the two nations to fight a long, costly war. The members of both governments knew it, and so did the generals and admirals. No matter how ludicrous the conflict seemed on the surface, the stakes were enormous.

"We fought," Pitt wrote, "for the control and domination of North America. We fought, as did the French, to determine which of us would win the richest prize on earth. We knew, as did the French, that the nation winning the New World would become the greatest and most powerful in the history of all civilization, greater than the empires of Alexander and Caesar."

The Spaniards had been the first to claim huge territories in the Americas. France had followed, during the reign of Henry IV, at the beginning of the seventeenth century. Smaller nations, among them Holland, Sweden, and Portugal, had entered the race, too, but had been forced out by the stronger powers of the Old World.

Great Britain had been the last to explore, to plant her flag, to send her sons across the Atlantic as colonists. Jamestown, in Virginia, had been an experiment. Many years passed before the settlement established there in 1607 really expanded. Most contemporary Englishmen never heard of the victims of religious persecution who went to Plymouth, in New England, in 1620, and those who did had little interest in whether or not they succeeded in creating a permanent foothold in the wilderness of America.

But many men in high places gradually became convinced of the importance of the New World. They provided ships and supplies, and offered financial bonuses to those who were willing to make new lives for themselves in the land where virgin forests stretched for thousands of miles.

By the middle of the seventeenth century, English settlers were coming to the New World in large numbers, often accompanied by their wives and children. Young men in search of adventure—and gold—came, too. So did those eager to undertake the challenge of exploration.

At the same time, the French were gradually building their own empire in what would become known as Canada. More realistic than the English, perhaps, they did not dream of discovering precious metals and gems. They knew that the real wealth of America lay in its furs, its unlimited supplies of timber, the riches of the land itself.

Between them, Great Britain and France forced an ever-weaker Spain out of the domain they themselves claimed. The two giants of western Europe staked out the better part of North America. "Our claims," Pitt wrote, "conflicted. It was inevitable that we should fight not one war, but many, until one or the other was forced to abandon the New World to the other."

By the eighteenth century, Great Britain was sending more immigrants to North America than was France. At the time the War of the Austrian Succession broke out, the population of the British colonies numbered approximately one million men, women, and children. Since New France had fewer than half that many settlers, the British appeared to possess an overwhelming advantage. But this was not the case.

Differences in colonial policy were responsible for balancing the scales more evenly. The French, from the outset, had consciously cultivated the friendship of the Indian tribes scattered throughout the wilderness. Where possible, they converted the Indians to Christianity. They paid them relatively high prices for furs and other goods. And they made it a rule to treat the Indians as equals.

The early English settlers, on the other hand, used their modern weapons, muskets and cannon, to drive out the Indians, to occupy their hunting and fishing grounds. They paid for furs and other goods only when necessary; in the main, they took what they wanted.

By 1740, the damage had been done. Although wiser, more enlightened British colonial administrators were try-

2

ing to repair the errors of the past and to win the friendship of the Indians, most of the tribes hated the English. But, almost without exception, the Indians considered the French their friends. So New France was able to rely on the help of skilled and ferocious warriors who had become their "natural allies," as Pitt ruefully called them.

The battle lines were drawn. What had started as an unprovoked attack by Frederick the Great on the Austrians in central Europe became a bitter colonial war, fought, many thousands of miles away, in the villages and towns that had been carved out of the North American wilderness. The formal marches and countermarches of handsomely uniformed European troops were thus intimately linked to the looting and burning, the kidnapping and scalping, that took place in the frontier settlements of Massachusetts Bay and Connecticut, New York and Pennsylvania and Virginia.

The real issues of what had begun as a strictly European conflict would be resolved in the vast forests of a still-primitive continent.

3

If most men in England and France failed to understand why their nations were at war with one another, there were few in the New World who long remained uncertain. In the spring and early summer of 1742, sporadic Indian attacks were directed against New Hampshire and Connecticut, Massachusetts Bay and its Maine District, which were among the colonies nearest to New France. Soon other areas began to be affected as well.

New York also lay close to Canada, but believed herself secure. After decades of unceasing warfare, she had finally established peaceful relations with her immediate neighbors, the powerful tribes of the Iroquois Confederation. There was no real friendship between the settlers and the Indians, to be sure, but each respected the other.

The attitude of New Yorkers was best expressed, perhaps, by Captain Alexander Dale, the deputy commander of Fort Albany, long the major frontier outpost on the upper reaches of the Hudson River. In a letter to his brother, who was studying medicine in Scotland, he wrote, "The frontier is quiet. The Seneca, Mohawk, and other nations of the Iroquois remain in their towns, and visit us only to trade. Just last week, a delegation came to the farm. Pa went for his rifle, but didn't need it. The Naturals wanted an iron skillet, and paid him three prime beaver pelts for it, a fair exchange.

"But we are not fooling ourselves. Two militia companies stand duty here at Fort Albany day and night, and the cannoneers sleep near their guns. If we were to give up this post, not one farm on the frontier would be safe. We know the Iroquois leave us unmolested only because they realize we will strike them doubly hard if they should assault us.

"So we stand fast, and peace is our reward!"

One night in July, 1742, Captain Dale and his men suffered a severe shock. A breathless teen-aged boy arrived at Fort Albany after traveling on foot more than twenty miles through the wilderness. He reported that his own family had been murdered by Indians, as had two neighboring families.

A general alarm was given, and two regiments of militiamen, all of them frontier settlers, immediately mustered at Fort Albany. Almost without exception the colonists assumed that their old enemies, the Mohawk and Seneca, had broken the truce.

Then a party of five senior warriors of the Seneca arrived at the post, led by Bear Tooth, eldest son of the tribe's sachem. Bear Tooth's message was plain: "No braves of the Iroquois have raised their hands against those who are protected by the guns of the soldiers. The braves of the Iroquois have not left their own towns."

Many militia officers and men refused to believe him. But no one could deny the logic of Captain Dale, who argued, "Bear Tooth would not have come to us if he were lying. He knows, as do all of the Seneca, that we would make him prisoner and kill him if the warriors of the Seneca or any other Iroquois tribe were molesting our settlers."

Soon scouts who lived in the wilderness, hunting game there when times were peaceful, brought word that Bear Tooth was telling the truth. The Indians who had attacked the remote farms had moved south from Canada and had escaped after murdering the settlers.

The entire colony of New York was in an uproar. Members of the Schuyler family, for many years among the most prominent citizens of the Fort Albany district, demanded that something be done at once. The most insistent was Philip Schuyler, who, a generation later, was to become a major general in the army that fought for America's independence from England.

"The invaders must be punished!" he declared in a pamphlet he wrote and published at his own expense. "New York cannot and must not tolerate wanton murder!"

Thousands of New Yorkers were in hearty agreement with him. Something had to be done. But what could the colony do? Its forests were enormous, and even if the regiments of militia were quadrupled, it would be impossible to patrol such a large area.

Perhaps the most startled of Americans were the citizens of Pennsylvania. Of all British colonies, it had enjoyed the greatest tranquillity. William Penn, founder of the colony, had made it his policy from the outset to win the friendship and respect of the local Indian tribes, and had succeeded brilliantly. Penn and his followers, who were members of the Society of Friends, familiarly known as Quakers, were opposed to violence. They had proved that the English were capable of establishing cordial relations with the Susquehannock and other local tribes.

Now, only a few weeks after the attacks near Fort Albany, Pennsylvanians suffered a similar fate. Two villages, one of them located only seventy-five miles west of the largest and most cultured of American cities, Philadelphia, were burned to the ground. There were no survivors.

An investigation of these tragedies established that the attacks had been made by Indians from Canada, who had been accompanied by French army officers. Stunned and fearful Pennsylvanians clamored for measures that would prevent a repetition of such outrages.

When news of the latest attacks spread through the English colonies, it was assumed that the marauders and the French officers in charge of the operation had returned to their bases in New France, as had been customary for Indian raiders in previous wars. But the assumption was mistaken.

Pioneers in Virginia who had moved from the seaboard to make their homes in the foothills of the Blue Ridge Mountains were the next to experience the savagery of an enemy determined to disrupt normal living in the English colonies through acts of terrorism.

The Blue Ridge pine forests had been part of the hunting grounds of the proud, stubborn Shawnee, one of the most highly developed and intelligent of the Indian nations. These Indians had developed a healthy respect for the marksmanship of the Virginia frontier dwellers. And the settlers, in turn, had learned they would not be molested if they treated the Shawnee fairly. Neither side had spoken to the other—there had been literally no communication between them, and there was no treaty or other formal understanding. Yet peace had prevailed in the Blue Ridge wilderness for almost twenty years. Settlers and savages alike worked to preserve the delicate balance, and when young hotheads on either side occasionally broke the peace, survivors of such encounters were chastised by older, wiser men on their own side.

Then, without warning, the Blue Ridge frontier erupted. The pattern was the same as it had been in other colonies. Hamlets and isolated farmhouses were subjected to surprise attacks, householders and their families were murdered and scalped, property was looted, and homes were burned to the ground.

The Shawnee, not wanting to be blamed, helped the frontier dwellers hunt down the raiders. Braves of the Shawnee nation and rifle-carrying woodsmen moved rapidly through territory with which they were thoroughly familiar. After a ceaseless search of two nights and a day they surprised a large party of alien Indians, and immediately attacked, although outnumbered by at least ten to one.

The Indians from New France had no desire to fight a battle if one could be avoided. In fact, it was later learned they were under orders not to engage in open combat. So they retreated, their superior strength enabling them to keep the Americans and Shawnee at a distance.

One of the Virginia marksmen managed to wound a member of the raiding party, however, and the man, unable to maintain the swift pace of his comrades, was abandoned by them. The Americans and Shawnee captured him, and were surprised to find he was actually a Frenchman who had disguised himself in war paint and buckskins.

Had there been a chance to question him at length, a great deal might have been learned about the future plans of the invaders. But the infuriated Blue Ridge settlers were far too angry to think in long-range terms. When they discovered their captive was a Frenchman, several rifles and pistols were simultaneously discharged, killing the prisoner instantly.

A great opportunity was lost, but no one blamed the men who had shot the captive. Tempers and tensions were so high that all Virginia demanded vengeance.

Not even South Carolina, situated far from New France, was spared. Warriors of the Creek nation, who had not taken to the warpath for almost a decade, began to raid the plantations and tiny villages of the west. South Carolina militiamen responded to the threat, and when an organized column marched against the main Creek towns, the Indians promptly asked for a truce. The Creeks, bewildered by the sudden reprisals, explained that they had been incited by Spaniards living in the Floridas. Intelligent men in Charleston quickly realized that the officials of New Spain, ordinarily timid and cautious, had been urged to break the peace by their mother country's ally, France.

In every English colony, there was an insistent demand for an end to the terror. Militia brigades, regiments, and battalions were formed, but the military leaders knew that the wilderness was too extensive for them to prevent a repetition of the attacks if they confined themselves to defensive warfare.

There were complications, too, that made it difficult for the English colonies to achieve their maximum potential strength. "Most of the tax money we raise is sent to England," Speaker Peter Livingston of the New York Assembly complained.

"England has promised to defend us," Judge Isaiah Harley of New Haven wrote. "Let her now keep her word."

Colonel Robert Henry Lee, commander of a regiment of Virginia light infantry, took a somewhat different view. "We're ready to defend ourselves," he said, "but our men need uniforms, weapons, ammunition, and provisions. We must rely on England to supply us with these sinews of war."

The governors of the colonies wrote to London, begging for assistance. There were few trained troops anywhere in the English colonies, they said, and although men like Colonel Lee were anxious to march off to war, New France was defended by professional soldiers. Therefore the English colonies had an urgent need for regiments of Regulars.

The ministers of King George II were acutely embarrassed. Great Britain, hard pressed to muster an army for service on the battlefields of Europe, could ill afford to provide her American colonies with either troops or funds. The high command in London made a study of the problem, and submitted its recommendations in an uncompromising report: "Not one platoon of troops can be spared for duty across the Atlantic. We will need all our troops for our campaigns on the Continent of Europe if we hope to conquer France."

The Royal Navy was somewhat more happily situated, and the admirals, after mulling the problem, finally sent a trim sloop of war off to the New World with a message.

Commodore Sir Peter Warren, a brilliant, energetic young officer, was the commander of a Royal Navy squadron that lay at anchor in the sultry harbor of Port Royal, on the southern shore of the island of Jamaica. His title, as he told friends with some amusement, was a grand one. He was "His Majesty's loyal commander in chief for the defense of the West Indian Islands." Now, late in 1742, when he received the message from the Admiralty in London, he was given a new and even more sweeping assignment. He was placed in charge of the naval defenses of all the English colonies of North America, and his fleet was ordered to cooperate fully with the governors of the various colonies.

Unfortunately for both Sir Peter and the colonies, his "fleet" consisted of precisely seven vessels, none of them ships of the line. Three, including his forty-four gun flagship, were frigates, which were swift and powerful, but were no match for huge ships of the line, which mounted twice as many guns and could blow them out of the water. The four smaller vessels of the squadron were sloops of war and schooners, which were useful in harassing civilian merchantmen, but would be ineffective in battle if a French fleet of any size should be encountered in the Atlantic.

Commodore Warren accepted his new task with the aplomb expected of a senior officer in the Royal Navy. He wanted to make certain his superiors understood his problems, however, and wrote to the Admiralty, "Your lordships are cognizant of the impossibility of one small squadron providing adequate protection for several thousand miles of colonial coastline. Fortunately, the admirals of the French fleet are somewhat lacking in imagination and daring. Therefore, I intend to patrol the customary shipping lanes, and with good luck may be able to help ward off a costly attack on Philadelphia, Charleston, New York Town, Boston, Newport, and other principal centers of population and commerce."

Warren was too efficient to trust to luck, however. As he sailed north from the Caribbean, he put into each of the main colonial ports, and there arranged with the owners of American and British merchantmen to keep him informed of any signs of the enemy that the masters of their ships might see in the Atlantic. With the aid of such "eyes," he reasoned, he might be able to ward off possible disaster.

His orders to his own captains were firm. "We shall make every attempt to find the enemy in the waters off North America," he wrote them, "and we shall sink him whenever our path crosses his."

When Sir Peter finally reached Boston, he found all of Massachusetts Bay in a ferment. Companies of infantry militia were marching and drilling in the Common, a cow pasture in the center of the city. The militia troops had erected their tents in the Common, too, even though the weather was very cold and damp, and they were prepared to endure any hardship for the sake of their colony's defense. The merchants who dined every afternoon at the Bunch o' Grapes, Boston's most distinguished tavern, were equally resolute. Their leader was a vigorous young international trader and ship owner, Thomas Hancock, whose nephew, John, would rise to prominence a generation later as the first signer of the Declaration of Independence, President of the Continental Congress, and Governor of Massachusetts Bay.

"A special tax should be levied on all imports and

exports," Hancock argued. "That will provide us with the revenues necessary to prosecute the war."

Hancock's plan was sound, and undoubtedly was inspired by patriotic motives. At the same time, however, he himself had nothing to lose by making the gesture, nor did his colleagues. Almost without exception, the wealthy citizens of Boston who engaged in trade were taking advantage of the absence of all but a single Royal Navy squadron in American waters, and were engaging in extensive smuggling activities. Although willing to pay a special tax for their own defense, they were reluctant to pay their normal export-import taxes, since these funds were being used to support Great Britain's war efforts in Europe, and were doing the colonies themselves little good.

Sir Peter was surprised by the extraordinary character of Governor William Shirley of Massachusetts Bay. Most colonial chief executives were incompetent men who were being rewarded for long and faithful service to the crown, men who knew little of the problems of the areas they were expected to administrate, and were content to accept the honors, but not the responsibilities, of their high posts.

The square-jawed Shirley was exceptionally able and energetic, and was completely devoted to the cause of Massachusetts Bay and her sister colonies. His letters to the Colonial Office in London, which was in charge of American affairs, invariably represented the local point of view, and King George II once remarked that "Shirley is the colonials' best spokesman." A generation later, John Adams, who was to become the second President of the United States, characterized Shirley as "the most remarkable British executive officer in the history of England's New World colonization."

It was Governor Shirley's contention that the current crisis created a situation unprecedented in American history. Until now, each colony had tried to stand alone, and rivalries between colonies had been intense. But the

French in Canada had no such problems, and their war efforts were being directed by a few men in Quebec who had been given great authority by their own superiors in Paris.

The time had come, Shirley believed, for the British colonies to band together, each voluntarily relinquishing some portion of its own cherished independence so that a unified effort to win the war could be made.

Sir Peter Warren agreed with Shirley, but doubted that other colonies, which resented the wealth and prestige of Massachusetts Bay, would accept any diminution of their own powers. However, he failed to take into account the intelligence and determination of the man who realized, more than anyone else in the English-speaking New World, that the French would win the war unless drastic measures were taken.

First, Shirley sent a blunt letter to the governors of the other colonies. "You and I," he wrote, "represent the same crown. It is madness for us to move in different, sometimes opposite, directions. We can safeguard the interests of His Majesty and discharge our obligations to the colonial peoples we represent only if we march together, in step."

His declaration seemed innocent enough, and, precisely as he had expected, the other governors wrote back to him, agreeing with the principle he had expressed. Now he was ready for the next step.

At his instigation, the Massachusetts Bay legislature passed a bill, which he immediately signed, increasing the colony's militia. Now there would be six full regiments of troops, four from Massachusetts Bay herself, and two from the Maine District. The legislature then voted a tax increase to support, feed, clothe, and arm these troops.

When this measure also had become law, Shirley sent another letter to his fellow governors, and at the same time, the legislature prepared a supporting declaration that was dispatched to the assemblies of the other colonies. In effect, Shirley and the Massachusetts Bay representatives were saying, "We're doing more than our fair share to defend our land. What are you doing?"

The other colonies, unwilling to be outstripped by the New England leaders, acted swiftly. Connecticut raised three regiments of soldiers, and created the first naval militia in America, converting several merchant ships into sloops of war. New Hampshire raised two regiments, New York created three, and so did Pennsylvania and Virginia. New Jersey and the Carolinas, which were thinly populated, had to be content with calling up battalions, units far smaller than regiments.

Only Rhode Island, the smallest of the colonies, balked. She had no western frontier and therefore saw no reason to raise any troops. What was more, she argued, Commodore Warren's squadron would protect her cities and coastal towns. But a wave of popular feeling forced her leaders to reverse their stand, and she, too, began to raise troops. Fiercely independent to the end, however, her assembly refused to set either a floor or a ceiling on the number of men to be called to duty. The size of the Rhode Island contingent would be determined exclusively by the number who volunteered for military service, be it one hundred or one thousand. Patriotic citizens flocked to the colors in huge numbers, and so many individuals pledged their financial support that Rhode Island was able to organize the only large body of artillery in the colonies worthy of the name. And, since there were few cannon in America, the Rhode Islanders ordered some made for them in England, then transported them to Newport, their principal seaport, in their own merchant ships.

In all, the British colonies had now mustered a force of more than five thousand men. And William Shirley, maneuvering constantly, had won the approval of his fellow governors, as well as the assemblies of the other colonies, for the use of these men in a joint enterprise. No official authorization for this purpose had been given, and none was actually needed. It was assumed that the various regiments and battalions would meet in Boston, and would engage in a joint enterprise of some sort.

It was also assumed that officers from Massachusetts Bay would be in command. However, Shirley took no chances, and after conferring with the key men in his own legislature, Massachusetts Bay gave the rank of Major General to the wealthy estate owner and merchant Colonel William Pepperrell, who had long been a student of war. At the same time the fiery Colonel Samuel Waldo of the Maine District was made a Brigadier General, and in addition to leading the troops from his own section of the country, was given the post of Pepperrell's deputy.

Since no other colony had the presence of mind to grant its senior officers rank higher than that of colonel, Pepperrell and Waldo automatically outranked everyone else. So, with a minimum of hard feelings, the problem of command was settled.

But a far larger question had not yet been resolved. Now that the Americans had a formidable army of their own, precisely how was this corps to be employed?

Some troops would be stationed on the western frontiers, of course, to guard against a repetition of the raids on wilderness settlements by the Indian allies of the French. But the colonels from New Hampshire and Connecticut, New York and Pennsylvania, Rhode Island and Virginia, who congregated in Boston, agreed with General Pepperrell and Governor Shirley that the best way to halt the assaults for all time would be to make a strong attack on New France itself.

Then the French would be too busy defending themselves to send out large parties of warriors to harass the colonists who lived across the border.

The logical target was Quebec, the capital of New France, a town that sat high on a bluff overlooking the broad St. Lawrence River. Commodore Warren, who returned from patrol duty at sea in order to take part in the discussions, doubted that such a campaign could succeed, and so did Pepperrell.

The obstacles seemed insurmountable. The troops would have to march hundreds of miles through the forests, some of them uncharted wilderness, in order to reach their goal. The French would learn of the impending attack from the Indians, and not only would have ample time to prepare their defenses, but could send out hundreds of warriors to attack the Americans in the dense forests.

Everyone who had any knowledge of wilderness fighting agreed that such a march would be suicidal. Losses on the march would be staggering, and it would be beyond the capacity of the supply masters to provide the corps with adequate food, clothing, cooking utensils, and other essentials on such an expedition.

Meeting in secret session behind closed doors several months before an expedition was actually formed, Commodore Warren, the two generals, and the colonels debated the issue. Governor Shirley, sheepishly admitting that he was an administrator and a statesman, not a soldier, announced that his own knowledge of military matters was too limited for him to suggest a solution. Tempers became frayed, and the result was a confused babble of conflicting opinions.

Shirley, more than any other man, kept the officers at their tasks, and they hated him for it. The fact that he was their intellectual superior and that he was still fresh when even the strongest of them became weary did nothing to endear him to them. Everyone admitted he was a brilliant administrator, but he could also be a petty tyrant and a boor. Yet, when men of substance were ready to walk out on him, he displayed his considerable charm, and they agreed to follow him again, to accept his suggestions, forgive his outbursts of bad temper, and above all, enjoy his lavish hospitality. Shirley was, in the words of a contemporary observer, "two-thirds Satan and one-third angel, but even his angelic qualities induce others to work all the harder for him."

The officers worked, but their discussions led nowhere. Ironically, the Americans had an army of their own at last, but there appeared to be no place to use it.

4

The friends and neighbors of Colonel William Vaughan, who regarded him with affectionate awe, sometimes doubted his sanity. As they put it, he had been "touched by the moon." Even the members of his own family were willing to concede that he was eccentric, and Vaughan, who enjoyed a good joke, frequently laughed at his own vagaries.

A graduate of Harvard College, he had returned to his native Maine District after completing his studies and promptly laid the foundations of a great fortune. Fish, he declared, were the source of the better part of the Maine District's income, and he therefore proposed that fishing be done on a more scientific basis.

He spent two years studying the habits of the codfish, often going to sea alone in a small boat for the purpose. At the end of that time, he had innumerable charts showing where the huge fish ran. He was willing to share his knowledge, he said, in return for a part interest in the efforts of others, and the fishermen who took the chance, using the data he gave them, found it surprisingly accurate.

Within a short time Vaughan owned a fishing fleet of his own, and it grew rapidly. The "Codfish King," as he was called, built himself a huge red brick mansion, had his clothes and those of his family made in Boston of the finest silks, and lived in a baronial style, often giving dinner parties that resembled ancient Roman feasts.

He never again put out in a fishing boat, confessing

that he became violently seasick. But the few who believed that a life of luxury had made him soft and who jeered him when he inspected the ships of his fleet, soon learned better. A violently aggressive man who kept himself in superb physical condition, he was more than a match in a fist fight, wrestling bout, or primitive free-for-all with the burliest of fishermen, dockhands, and carpenters.

"I ask no man to respect my accomplishments, my wealth, or my person," he wrote on one occasion to his elder son when the boy was attending Harvard. "But I demand that every man respect the power of my fists."

As a hobby, Vaughan studied the military campaigns of Julius Caesar and other ancient Roman and Greek military leaders. He was a superb horseman and an excellent pistol shot, and he wielded a sword with such easy grace that no one had ever dared challenge him to a duel. Since he was also an acknowledged leader of men, it was inevitable, perhaps, that he should have been granted a colonel's commission by the Massachusetts Bay legislature and made the commander of the First Regiment of Maine District Foot.

Codfish King Vaughan sat through the long debates of his colleagues in Boston, becoming increasingly restless and bored with their discussions. Finally, unable to tolerate the interminable talk any longer, he decided to do something about the matter. The action he took was typical of him, and the memorandum he submitted to the Commodore, General Pepperrell, General Waldo, and his fellow colonels created an instant sensation.

"I propose," he wrote, "that we reduce, capture, and occupy the enemy fortress of Louisburg."

Commodore Warren and General Pepperrell were stunned, General Waldo laughed aloud at the utter absurdity of the suggestion, and the other colonels were convinced that Vaughan was indeed mad.

Louisburg was the strongest of all fortresses in the

New World, and there were many who believed it had no rival in Europe or elsewhere in the civilized world. Its strategic importance was enormous. It was located on Cape Breton Island, a small, rocky body of land between Nova Scotia and Newfoundland, and guarded not only the Gulf of St. Lawrence, but the St. Lawrence River itself. It was the sentinel that stood sentry duty over all of New France, and its location alone made it a permanent threat to the British colonies, which would never be secure as long as French warships could find shelter in its harbor protected by the mighty guns of the fort.

The great pile of massive stone was tribute to the foresight and hard labor of a nation determined to entrench itself in the New World. Until 1720, Cape Breton Island had been the home of a few enterprising farmers who raised sheep and cattle, braving the heat of blistering summers and chilling winters. In that year, work began on a series of buildings and ramparts, consisting of walls within walls, inner forts surrounded by what had become one of the most heavily fortified towns ever constructed by civilized man.

French taxpayers sometimes complained that work on Louisburg would never be finished. They were right. The fort was a challenge to every engineer and general in the French army, and by the time the Seven Years' War broke out, more than thirty million livres in gold had been spent on it. This sum, the equivalent of more than ten million dollars in the latter part of the twentieth century, was more than any nation had ever poured into a defense fortification.

"Capture Louisburg," an English general said in 1738 after catching a glimpse of the place from the outside, "and you capture Canada."

He was mocking himself and his fellow countrymen when he made the remark. The very idea of trying to reduce Louisburg was preposterous. King Louis XV, after whom it was named, aptly called it "the largest and most invulnerable ship of the line on the high seas." Although he had never seen it himself, he knew enough of war to recognize its worth.

Louisburg was designed to be self-sustained and self-sustaining. According to the available information, there was enough grain, salt fish, and smoked meat in the rock-hewn cellars to feed a large garrison for months. But presumably the fort had no need to depend on her emergency rations alone. Cape Breton Island was one hundred and ten miles long, and, at her deepest point, approximately eighty-six miles wide. Local farmers, although very poor, were thought to be capable of providing the troops with fresh meat and vegetables, poultry and butter and cereals, in return for French gold. And nowhere in the New World was there better fishing, as William Vaughan knew. Cod abounded in the cold waters off the island's shores, as did tuna and smaller fish. More than 1,500,000 fish were caught each year off her coasts.

The site of the fort had been selected by men endowed with genius. Even in the coldest weather, the water, protected by land on all sides except for a narrow channel, did not freeze. The waters of the harbor were deep enough to accommodate the largest ships afloat, yet the entrance was so narrow that admission could be barred by cannon on both sides.

It was reported that Louisburg was large enough to accommodate comfortably a garrison of as many as twenty thousand officers and men. However, no one knew precisely how many troops were stationed there. The exact number was one of the most closely guarded of France's military secrets.

Some facts, though, were obvious to the British officers who had sailed past the place in small boats, disguised as fishermen. The outer walls were made of huge blocks of stone four feet high and four feet wide. No cannon on earth could smash them. And the walls of the inner, star-shaped fort, where a last-ditch defense could be made if an enemy miraculously managed to breach the outer line, were even thicker.

According to the intelligence reports that had reached London and, eventually, Boston, Louisburg boasted at least fifty twenty-four-pounder cannon, the largest guns ever made. And she was armed with so many smaller guns, some of them concealed in turrets and behind ramparts, that no outsider had ever been able to count them.

The Marquis de Moriceau, a former commandant of the fort, had visited London after his retirement from the French army, and had freely told friends that he, his wife, and their five children had lived in quarters far more spacious than they would have found in any palace or chateau in France. Other officers also lived in sumptuous apartments, and there was a fully equipped hospital within the walls, as well as a school for the children of gentlemen, a small theater, and many other refinements of civilization.

Instead of being equipped with a single set of iron gates, like most forts, Louisburg had three, the outermost of stone, the next of iron, and the inner set of oak. No one except qualified French military men had ever stepped inside the thick wooden gates that guarded the core of Louisburg. The Marquise de Moriceau complained rather bitterly that she had been barred. The sachems of the Abnaki, Algonkin, Micmac, and other Indian tribes who were allies of the French and who came to Louisburg for powder, weapons, and ammunition were also denied entrance to the inner fort, even though they were highly sensitive to slights.

It was said, jokingly, that King Louis himself would have difficulty proving his right to go unchallenged past the wooden doors. And although no one knew for certain,

it was rumored that several British and American espionage
agents had been hanged after being caught trying to
penetrate to Louisburg's heart.

A commission composed of some of Great Britain's
highest-ranking generals and admirals made a study of
Louisburg's defenses shortly after the outbreak of the
Seven Years' War, based on their admittedly incomplete
military information. Even the fragments at hand convinced them that an attack on the fort, no matter how
strong or how heavily supported, would inevitably fail.

Commodore Sir Peter Warren was not only familiar with
the recommendation, but actually had read its conclusions
to the colonial officers gathered in Boston. Less than two
weeks had passed since this sobering information had been
passed along, and none of the officers had forgotten any
of the grim details.

It was small wonder, then, that those who were attending the secret meetings were convinced that Codfish
King Vaughan had lost his senses.

If the royal commission had rejected the idea of British
Regulars, escorted by a powerful fleet, attacking Louisburg, how could colonial amateurs take the fortress? The
majority of militiamen had never fired a musket or rifle
in battle, and the only ships available for escort purposes
would be Warren's own small squadron. The attempt, the
Commodore said, would be disastrous.

William Vaughan refused to back down. He was aware
of the hazards, he said cheerfully, but felt certain they
could be overcome. Wasn't it true, he asked Warren, that
the French fleet was busy in European waters, trying to
maintain a defense against the larger, more powerful
British navy?

Warren had to admit that, in all probability, there were
few French warships stationed at Louisburg.

Vaughan then turned to General Pepperrell. Wasn't it

true, he demanded, that Louisburg was the very last place the French expected an attack?

The commander in chief of the American forces had to concede that the French wouldn't dream of such an assault.

Wasn't it also true, the mettlesome Maine District officer wanted to know, that surprise attacks on forts usually enjoyed the greatest success?

Again Pepperrell reluctantly agreed.

By now, others were becoming interested in the idea. It was so daring that many of the officers were intrigued, in spite of themselves, and even Pepperrell and Warren, the two men whose word would be final, had fallen thoughtfully silent.

At the worst, Colonel Vaughan continued, an expedition would be driven off. If it appeared that losses would be heavy, the British-American flotilla could retreat. He was so convinced the chances of victory were good, however, that he offered the use of the largest and sturdiest fishing vessels in his fleet as troop transports.

By now the members of the war council were taking the proposal seriously. If Vaughan was willing to risk the loss of expensive fishing schooners that could not be replaced in wartime, it was apparent that he had weighed the odds and found them favorable.

Governor Shirley, unlike the military men, had not yet recovered from his initial astonishment. Was there really a possibility, he asked, that Louisburg could be captured?

Pepperrell replied in a brief address that was transcribed by his aides. When published several years later, it won him lasting renown in military circles. "Any defenses erected by man can be destroyed by man," he said. "Intelligent planning, careful execution of that plan, consistent demonstrations of courage by the offensive corps, and sound leadership can achieve any goal, provided the initial considerations are realistic. It would be absurd for one hundred men to attack a strong fort defended by one thousand, but those same one hundred might have a far better chance if the fort were held by a like number."

General Waldo asked for the floor. Silent throughout the debate, this soft-spoken man who had made his fortune shipping prime timber to England was farsighted. And, in spite of his unquestioned personal valor, which he had shown many times in frontier fights with the Algonkin, he was no military radical. The dispatch of an expedition to Louisburg, he declared, depended on the size of the French garrison there. If the fort was heavily manned, the idea should be dropped at once. If, however, it was lightly held, the scheme should be given further consideration.

Again Colonel Vaughan stood, and there was a ring of triumph in his voice as he produced several documents from the inner pocket of his blue uniform tunic. He had acquired proof, he said, that the French garrison was undermanned. Just as Great Britain was having trouble finding enough men to serve in Europe, and hence could not send troops to the New World, so was France vexed by the same problem. In fact, several thousand veterans who had been stationed on Cape Breton Island had recently been withdrawn and transferred to Europe.

Fewer than three thousand men now held the great fort. They were seasoned troops of the regular French military establishment, and therefore knew how to fight, but their ranks had been thinned. And it was unlikely that the garrison would be reinforced, unless, of course, the French learned that an expedition would be sent from Boston to take Louisburg.

There was an immediate clamor. Everyone wanted an explanation of the so-called proof.

Vaughan gave the documents to General Pepperrell and Commodore Warren. They were letters from one of his closest and most trusted associates, the master of a fishing schooner who had been in business with him for more than twenty years. This man, Jean Duval, was a native of Paris who had come to New France in his teens. But, after spending several years in Quebec, he had been a participant in a tavern brawl in which a man had died. Duval had fled to the Maine District, where he now made his home.

At Vaughan's instigation he had gone to Cape Breton Island, posing as the master of a French fishing vessel, and had spent the better part of two weeks there. During that time he had made discreet but careful inquiries of farmers and shop owners, and had also chatted at length with a number of French officers on the staff of the garrison, whom he had met at a Louisburg tavern.

Among them had been a major and two captains. He had spent separate evenings with each, and after treating them to potent concoctions of brandywine and rum, they had spoken freely to him. Each had told him the garrison had been cut down to a meager force of twenty-nine hundred men. And all were bitter, believing that the high command in Paris was more concerned about the war in Europe than about the fate of the greatest fortress in the New World.

The Americans could sympathize with the feelings of the frustrated French officers. But they had no way of knowing whether they could take Duval at his word. The letters the fishing schooner master had written contained invaluable information, but was he telling the truth?

Colonel Vaughan vouched for his friend without qualification, saying he would trust Jean Duval as completely as he would trust anyone in the council chamber, including his old friend and neighbor, General Waldo. There was no doubt in his mind that the data given him by Duval was authentic, and the others could prove to their own satisfaction that the schooner master was telling the truth by taking part in an expedition to Louisburg.

3

The meeting adjourned for twenty-four hours to let the officers think about the problem. During that time, Commodore Warren and the two generals questioned Vaughan repeatedly, and he told them many intimate details of Jean Duval's life. By the time he was finished, they shared his conviction that the news the schooner master had brought back to the Maine District from Cape Breton Island was indeed as accurate as information obtained by any espionage agent could be.

The temptation to lead an expedition against the fortress was great. In fact, the high-ranking officers realized that the capture of Louisburg would be such a crushing blow to New France that it would end the war in the New World.

But a number of obstacles were still in the way. Commodore Warren said it was possible that a squadron of French warships larger than his own command might be lurking somewhere in American waters. If it appeared after a landing was made on the island, bottling up the attackers, the Americans and his own squadron would be caught between the fire of the land-based guns and the cannon mounted on warships.

He was willing to take that risk, however, believing that his own gunners were sufficiently accomplished to break a blockade. The Commodore's convictions were so strong that he put them in writing, sending a full report to the Admiralty in London.

General Pepperrell also entertained genuine fears. Approximately four thousand troops were available to take part in the expedition, with another one thousand remaining behind to guard the frontier settlements. In theory, at least, the Americans would enjoy a distinct numerical advantage over the defenders of the fort. But the militiamen were amateur soldiers. Even those accustomed to the hardships of wilderness living had never been subjected to rigorous military disciplines, and no corps could hope to take a stronghold as well-defended as Louisburg unless strict discipline was maintained at all times.

There were other, more subtle problems that had to be considered, too. Never before had men from various colonies worked and fought together. The Pennsylvanians and New Yorkers were jealous of Massachusetts Bay. The Virginians kept to themselves, and others resented them, considering them too clannish. Men from Connecticut despised the stubborn Rhode Islanders, and troops from New Hampshire thought of anyone living in the Maine District as a member of an inferior breed.

Would it be possible to persuade, cajole, and direct the men from the different colonies to forget their rivalries and cooperate with each other? No one could prophesy how they might react under the strain of a difficult campaign, and in the heat of battle.

General Waldo wondered whether enough supplies could be carried to support a corps of four thousand men for many weeks, perhaps months. The supply masters were called in, but they could give no definitive answers to the question. None had ever handled such a vast task, and the best these officers could do was to promise they would try.

Then Governor Shirley, always aware of delicate political situations, brought up a matter that startled the military men. Each colony would be required to grant permission for its own troops to leave British territory for operations on foreign soil. And when the governors and assemblies of the other colonies learned that the goal was Louisburg, each would demand the right to lead the expedition in order to obtain the lion's share of the glory. It was certain there would be jealous squabbling, and the secret would leak out. When that happened, the French would reinforce Louisburg, virtually guaranteeing the expedition's failure.

Pepperrell, Warren, and Waldo were incapable of finding a solution. But the astute William Shirley solved the dilemma himself. He proposed that the military leaders of each colony be sent back to their governors and assembly chiefs with a confidential, verbal message. Massachusetts Bay, they would tell their civilian superiors, was planning to conduct a campaign against Louisburg, and each of the other colonies was being invited to join the expedition. This simple expedient automatically eliminated wrangles over leadership, and also reduced to the essential minimum the number of people who would know the expedition's object.

Another meeting of the colonels from all the colonies was called, and General Pepperrell asked for a vote. The officers were unanimously in favor of sailing to Louisburg and investing the fort.

The council of war adjourned, and the colonels returned to the capitals of their own colonies. It was taken for granted that French espionage agents were stationed in Boston, Philadelphia, and the other major cities of the British colonies. So it was probable that word of the meeting would be sent to Quebec.

But for the present, at least, the French had no idea what decisions had been reached at the council. Elaborate precautions were taken to make certain that the enterprise remain secret. The colonels played their parts brilliantly, requiring their governors and legislature leaders to take an oath before hearing the news. Also, no military personnel below the rank of full colonel were told the war plans.

One by one, the colonies sent word back to Governor Shirley, accepting the invitation of Massachusetts Bay to take part in the expedition. The great enterprise was at last beginning to gather momentum.

5

The assignment undertaken by Brigadier General Samuel Waldo in the autumn of 1744 was unique in the history of New World warfare. First, he was directed to prevent the authorities in Quebec from learning that the British colonies were going to send an expedition into New France. Waldo knew, as did General Pepperrell and Commodore Warren, who had given him the order, that only a miracle would keep the French completely in the dark.

Every colony accepted the invitation of Massachusetts Bay to take part in the campaign. And in every colony, unprecedented military preparations were being made. Militiamen drilled daily in town greens and village squares, and recruiting sergeants constantly sought replacements for the incompetent and fainthearted, who were inactivated. It was obvious to any French agent traveling through the English colonies that something out of the ordinary was being planned.

So Waldo prepared an elaborate deception. Enemy spies who refused to believe that the regiments of infantry, batteries of artillery, and squadrons of artillery were being trained for the defense of the American frontier would be led to think that an overland march against Quebec was being contemplated. Lieutenant colonels, majors, and company-grade officers of the militia were told they might take part in an attack on the capital of New France, and soon the word seeped down to the enlisted men and their families.

The expedition's real goal remained a secret held by only a handful of the most responsible civilian and military officials. All of them realized the campaign would fail, at a cost of many lives, if the truth became known. So the governors and top militia commanders did everything in their considerable power to help Waldo deceive the enemy. No matter how great or how complicated the effort, it was imperative that the French be given no hint that Louisburg would be the target of the American corps. The governors and colonels responded superbly. They were so close-mouthed, in fact, that Anne Vaughan, the wife of the man who had sparked the campaign, wrote a letter to her sister, in Boston, complaining that "William tells me nothing of his intentions in the spring. All I know is that he will absent from home for a long period."

Realizing it would be virtually impossible to keep secret the gathering of provisions, the supply masters of each regiment openly purchased food, blankets, tents, and munitions. Warehouses were leased in every major town, and in them were stored the many items the troops would need. Sacks of parched corn and of wheat were piled high. So were sides of smoked beef and venison, kegs of salt pork, barrels of pickled fish, and such delicacies as dried prunes and chopped nuts. Bolts of wool, which were used for blankets, and canvas, which was made into tents, disappeared from the shelves of many merchants.

There was also a shortage of iron kettles and skillets, spades and picks and axes, as well as of such civilian essentials as needles and thread. A French espionage agent would have to be practically blind, General Waldo admitted, not to know that the Americans were planning a major move of some sort.

But great precautions were taken to prevent the enemy from discovering that these supplies were transferred, a little at a time, to the minor American seaports, such as New London, in Connecticut, Southampton, on Long

Island, Marblehead, in Massachusetts Bay, and Sakonnet, in Rhode Island.

Seemingly innocent ships put in at these ports, among them the merchantmen owned by Thomas Hancock of Boston, and the fishing schooners of William Vaughan. In all, a fleet of more than forty vessels was gathered at the various ports, the owners contributing their ships without knowing where they would be sailing.

Commodore Warren, who was in charge of the naval operations, transferred his own headquarters from Boston to New York Town, and put out to sea each week on a short cruise, ostensibly searching for enemy squadrons. What he actually did, however, was to travel from one of his ports of embarkation to another, always going ashore from the least conspicuous of his own warships, a small sloop.

The cannon that the militia artillery batteries intended to use caused him many sleepless nights, but he finally worked out a system for loading them without the knowledge of enemy spies. The guns were carted, one by one, to a deserted section of Connecticut beach on Long Island Sound, where some of Warren's own Royal Navy seamen, disguised as fishermen, stood guard over them. Then, late one dark night in the winter of 1744–45, two of the squadron's frigates dropped anchor in the Sound, and sent their longboats ashore. The guns were hauled on board, and from there were transferred to the frigates.

Marines were posted on sentry duty to keep strangers from approaching the area, and the operation was completed before daybreak. No one but Warren's own men took part in the loading and moving of the guns, so he felt reasonably sure that no one in the employ of the French knew what he had done.

General Waldo was also charged with the responsibility of keeping watch on the enemy to find out whether Louisburg was reinforced. He used a number of small fishing boats from the Maine District for the purpose. The masters of these little craft, often accompanied by crews of only two or three men, patrolled the shipping lanes in the Atlantic that led to Cape Breton Island. Their task was hazardous, but simple. They were directed to report to Waldo without delay all ship movements, particularly of troop transports.

These scouts were among the unsung heroes of the rapidly developing campaign. Men in tiny, frail craft braved icy weather and rough seas for many days at a time, and accepted their difficult work without complaint. There were other dangers as great as the weather, too. A French frigate, sailing to Cape Breton Island, trained her guns on one fishing boat, forced her to halt, and took her master on board for questioning. He was released after being warned not to fish in French waters.

The Atlantic belonged to no nation, and the master of the fishing boat expressed his indignation in such forceful language that the French frigate captain threatened to confiscate his boat and take him and his crew to Louisburg in irons. By this time the wily fisherman had learned all he wanted to know: The frigate carried no one on board but her usual crew.

As soon as he was released, he headed for Kittery, in the Maine District, to tell General Waldo of his experience. Four weeks later, the same frigate was seen sailing in the opposite direction, toward Europe, and the fishing boat master who sighted her was able to escape without being apprehended.

Several others were less fortunate. One fishing craft disappeared without a trace during a violent mid-winter storm. Another was taken in tow by a French sloop of war, and was last seen sailing toward Louisburg. No one ever learned what became of her master and his two companions. Their boat vanished, too, in one of the strangest tragedies of the war. In fact, when inquiries were pressed years later, after the war had ended, the French Admiralty denied all knowledge of the affair.

While others made physical preparations for the expedition, General Pepperrell and his staff spent a frantically busy autumn and winter at a solitary farmhouse they rented outside the little town of Braintree, not far from Boston. There they made their plans for the landing on Cape Breton Island and the investment of the fortress.

They were hampered by a lack of information about Louisburg. How large was the fort? How high were its walls? Where were its strong points? Where were its heaviest cannon emplaced?

Only one man was in a position to provide them with some of the answers to their questions. Jean Duval, the fishing-fleet owner from the Maine District who had spent many days on Cape Breton Island, was invited to the Massachusetts Bay farmhouse.

He drew crude sketches and patiently tried to find adequate replies to the many questions that Pepperrell and his aides asked. But it soon became evident that Duval, although a student of human nature, was woefully ignorant of military matters. He had seen the walls of Louisburg, to be sure, and guessed they were about twenty feet high, but could not be certain. To the best of his recollection, the outer bastions were star-shaped, but he had not paid that much attention to them. And he had no idea where the cannon, large or small, were located. All he could say was that the fort was bristling with them.

Duval went back to his own home, chagrined, as he later wrote to Colonel Vaughan, that he been able to "contribute so little to a sacred cause." Apparently he failed to realize that the superb espionage work he had done was making the expedition possible.

William Pepperrell was an exhaustively thorough, patient man, as the members of his staff were able to testify by the end of the grueling winter. Because his knowledge of Louisburg was limited, the commander in chief could not satisfy himself with one or two sets of plans; he made scores of them. He had to be completely prepared for every conceivable contingency, and detailed operational procedures were drawn up for each.

These plans, which were carefully numbered, contained instructions for every regimental commander, yet allowed these unit heads enough latitude to deal with emergencies as they saw fit. Copies were made by the two young lieutenants who were Pepperrell's personal aides, and a separate packet was prepared for every senior officer who would sail on the expedition.

Pepperrell would have achieved lasting renown had he done nothing but draw up these contingency plans. They were such models of operational thinking that they were used as texts in the military academies of Great Britain, the United States, and a number of European nations as much as one hundred years later.

The militiamen from Virginia, who had the farthest distance to travel, were the first to move. They marched north to the little port of New Castle, Delaware, where they and the troops from Pennsylvania embarked on brigs, large fishing boats, and several rugged but clumsy vessels that were used for carrying lumber and other heavy merchandise up and down the seaboard.

Commodore Warren was on hand for the embarkation, as he was for each of the others up the coast, making certain that nothing went amiss. His own squadron put out to sea without him, and the transports, unguarded, sailed north toward a secret rendezvous. This was one of the most dangerous phases of the entire operation. If attacked by French warships, the transports would be helpless. But Warren preferred the risk to that of sailing in a large convoy, as the French might guess their enemy's plans if they sighted one huge flotilla moving north.

The naval commander in chief did not transfer to his own flagship, the *Superbe*, until the British warships reached a point about fifty miles off the port of Boston. When he finally went on board the frigate, he learned that all phases of the embarkation were proceeding smoothly. The squadron of naval militia from Connecticut had sailed without incident, as had another unit of converted brigs and merchant sloops from Massachusetts Bay. Seamen from Boston and other ports in the colony, unable to tolerate the idea that Connecticut alone had her own navy, had armed seven of their own vessels.

General Pepperrell and his staff were on board the colony's flagship the *Massachusetts*, a former brig, which now carried twenty-four cannon and, technically, qualified as a frigate. The commander of the American sub-squadron was Captain Edward Tyng of Marblehead, a veteran sailor who had once held a commission in the Royal Navy, and who therefore was better qualified to understand and interpret Commodore Warren's orders than were other American naval officers, whose experience at sea had been exclusively civilian.

The militiamen and colonial naval units sailed without fanfare. Nowhere were there parades, or addresses by either governors or local officials. A fife and drum corps had appeared at the little port of Sakonnet, Rhode Island, intending to serenade the departing troops, but had been dispersed by the militia commanders.

The first troops to go to sea had left New Castle, Delaware, on March 1, 1745, and the last to sail was the New Hampshire contingent, which put out of Portsmouth on March 24. Two days later all of the ships converged on the tiny fishing town of Kittery, Maine, where General Waldo lived and where General Pepperrell had made his home before moving to Boston. Only when vessel after vessel dropped anchor in the crowded harbor did men begin to realize the staggering magnitude of the operation.

Commodore Warren commanded twenty warships, including his own squadron of seven, another seven from Massachusetts Bay, and six from Connecticut. But what really astonished the militiamen was the number of transports that moved into the harbor, more than ninety in all.

The troops of Colonel Vaughan's regiment formed a tight sentry cordon around Kittery, keeping out all strangers and forbidding residents of outlying areas who had no legitimate business in the town to pass their lines. The officers of the high command held a meeting that began early on the morning of March 27 and lasted late into the night. Meanwhile, the crews of the ships went ashore for supplies of fresh water. The troops, however, were restricted to their transports, which caused considerable grumbling.

Then, on the morning of March 28, General Pepperrell and Commodore Warren ordered all military and naval personnel ashore for a review and inspection. The day was dark and gloomy, the damp air was chilling, and during the parade, which was held in an open area near the shipbuilding yards, a light snow began to fall. Finally, after every unit had passed the reviewing stand, General Pepperrell ordered all men to move closer, within the sound of his voice.

"This corps of courageous Englishmen and brave American colonials," he said, "has a glorious destiny. We are going to capture the strongest fortress on earth, Louisburg!"

There was a moment of stunned silence, and then bedlam broke out. Men cheered until they were hoarse, and a regiment of exuberant Pennsylvanians threw their stocking caps into the air. (The Pennsylvanians subsequently regretted their impulsive act, as they had some trouble recovering their headgear, which scattered over a wide area.)

General Pepperrell went on to make a short, pungent

address. The idea of attacking the great French fort had been under consideration for more than a year, he declared, and every precaution had been taken to safeguard the lives of the soldiers and sailors who would participate in the campaign. But he wanted no one to suffer from false impressions.

The investment would be long and tedious, difficult and costly. The campaign would consist of several, distinct phases. First, it would be necessary to make a landing and gain a foothold on Cape Breton Island. Men would die in the effort.

Second, it would be essential to silence enough enemy guns to insure the warships and transports of safe berths. Men would die, and ships might be sunk.

Third, siege lines would be established, and would be moved closer to the fort, little by little. No military effort was as trying as a siege, which required stamina and patience. General Pepperrell admitted he had no idea how long the investment might last, and he made no glib promises of an early, easy victory. If the French held out for a considerable period, food supplies might begin to run short, and in that event it would be necessary to put everyone on half rations. So it was possible, if not probable, that everyone would grow hungry before the campaign finally came to an end.

The last phase of the operation would be the most perilous. When the siege became virtually unendurable, and the French began to waver, an assault would be made on the fort. Men would run across open, unprotected ground, braving the musket and cannon fire of the defenders, in an attempt to scale Louisburg's high walls.

If one such assault failed, another would be made, then still another, until the enemy at last surrendered. Such attacks required the ultimate in courage. Many men would die, many others would be wounded.

A surgeon was traveling with every battalion, and large stocks of medicines, unguents, and poultices were being carried in battalion and regimental supplies. Nevertheless, men would suffer. The cost of victory would be high.

The troops listened in sober silence as the commander in chief realistically outlined what was ahead. There were no cheers now, and no smiles. Every man standing in the cold on the Kittery waterfront knew he would be subjected to hazards greater than any he had ever faced.

General Pepperrell concluded his speech with an extraordinary statement. Since the soldiers and sailors had not known the destination of the expedition, he believed it unfair to force anyone to fight against his will. Some might agree with the French, who had been boasting for almost a quarter of a century that no enemy could take their great fort. Some might believe the odds against survival too high.

Therefore, Pepperrell said, any man who did not want to participate in the campaign would be excused, allowed to return to his own home without a black mark of any kind on his record. Those who wanted discharges from their obligations were directed to report at once to their regimental commanders or ship captains, who would remain on shore for the purpose of accepting such resignations. The others were ordered to return at once to their transports.

The next hour was critical. The idea of allowing reluctant men to withdraw from the enterprise had been Pepperrell's, and his immediate subordinates had protested strongly when he had told them of his plan. Commodore Warren had been dubious, too, saying that so many men might resign that the entire expedition would founder.

But General Pepperrell had remained adamant. Louisburg, he had said, could be taken only if everyone participating in the enterprise believed wholeheartedly that the campaign would succeed. So many trials and hardships lay ahead that a handful of disaffected men would influence others. The dissatisfaction would spread, and the effort to capture the fort would fail. Therefore, he reasoned, it would be far better to sail with a smaller force made up of men determined to achieve victory.

The results of Pepperrell's surprising offer exceeded the expectations of every member of the high command. Only eleven militiamen, including one junior officer, expressed the desire to return home, and the three naval militiamen who resigned changed their minds when they discovered that all of their colleagues were going to see the campaign through to the end.

General Waldo, Commodore Warren, and the colonels agreed that General Pepperrell's generous offer had given the expedition the sudden lift in spirits that was essential to its success. Every man taking part in the campaign could, with propriety, call himself a volunteer, and could feel a justified sense of pride in his own role.

Sir Peter offered Pepperrell and Waldo quarters on board the *Superbe,* or if they preferred, either of his other frigates, the *Mermaid* or the *Eltham.* However, the commander in chief deemed it wiser to travel on board Captain Tyng's flagship, the *Massachusetts,* so the troops would know he was willing to take the same risks to which they were exposed. Ordinarily he and his deputy would have sailed on board the same ship, but there was a strong possibility that a converted brig might be sunk if any French warships appeared to contest the approach of the flotilla to Louisburg. So General Waldo was given a small suite of cabins on the *Connecticut,* thus insuring that the corps would have a commander, even if one or the other American warship was destroyed.

The fleet planned to put out to sea on the night of March 28, but a sudden storm blew up, holding the expedition at Kittery for an additional three days. Parson Samuel Moody of the Maine District, the corps' senior chaplain, took advantage of the delay and held an almost continuous series of prayer meetings, which were so well-attended that, for the first time in his life, he lost his voice.

The men were allowed to write to their families now, telling wives and parents the destination of the corps, and thousands of letters were turned over to the Kittery post-master, who had never before been so inundated. It was impossible to keep the secret from the citizens of the little town, of course, and on March 31, they made a farewell gesture of their own.

Fishermen contributed catches of cod and tuna, as well as of bluefish and other smaller fish. Lobster pots were emptied, and the children of the town went out into the rain to search for oysters and clams on the beaches. Then the women of Kittery cooked huge batches of fish chowder in their largest kettles, adding potatoes, corn, and onions to the dish.

Steaming kettles were carried out to the transports, where the men ate the last civilian meal they would enjoy for many months.

Around ten o'clock in the evening, the weather began to clear, and Commodore Warren alerted the captains of all ships, ordering them to be prepared to sail at any time. Shortly before midnight the stars appeared, the wind shifted, and there was no reason to delay any longer.

Parson Moody, who was traveling with General Pepperrell on the *Massachusetts*, offered a prayer, and the commander in chief stood bareheaded on the main deck, as did the officers and men of the Massachusetts Bay flagship.

A few moments later word was passed from one ship to another: "Hoist anchors and set sails!"

Slowly the armada nosed out of the Kittery harbor into the open Atlantic, the British sloops in the van, followed by the *Superbe*, the *Massachusetts*, and the *Connecticut*.

The transports were strung out across the sea in a long line, with the other warships riding herd on their flanks, shepherding them back into their places when they strayed.

Bringing up the rear was the most powerful of the American vessels, the *New Haven*, a brig of four hundred and fifty tons that now carried thirty-six cannon. She held a place of honor, but her sailors were disgruntled, fearing they would miss any action that might take place.

The fleet tacked, setting a course for the northeast, and five thousand Englishmen and American colonials started on the last leg of their mission.

General Pepperrell, conscious of the terrible weight of responsibility he carried, was unable to sleep, and paced up and down the open deck of the *Massachusetts*, apparently unmindful of the raw cold that numbed the hands and feet of the watch officers and helmsmen. Although his aides worried about his health, they were afraid to interrupt him and urge that he go to bed.

At dawn, the lookouts climbed to the crow's-nests, high above the rigging, and General Pepperrell looked across the water at the *Superbe*, a short distance away. There, on the quarterdeck of the fleet's flagship, also pacing restlessly, was Sir Peter Warren.

The two men on whose shoulders rested the future of the English-speaking people in the New World exchanged salutes and waves. Each knew how the other felt. It was impossible to relax, even though the long months of planning and preparation were at an end. Within a short time one of the great issues of the age would be decided, and either Great Britain or France would rule the New World.

6

The first days of the voyage passed without incident. The sea was calm, the winds were favorable, and the transports held their assigned places in the line, thanks to the almost superhuman efforts of the captains of the Royal Navy ships. When the flotilla was less than forty-eight hours from her goal, several small fishing boats were sighted, but these vessels promptly fled toward the south. Since they sailed more slowly than the flotilla, Commodore Warren knew it would be impossible for them to double back and reach Louisburg in time to warn the defenders of the threat.

On the morning of April 12, 1745, the fleet of more than one hundred and ten ships approached Gabarus Bay on the southeastern shore of Cape Breton Island. Sails were trimmed so the ships would not reach their destination before daybreak, and Sir Peter's timing was perfect. As the first streaks of light appeared in the sky, the British frigates, now massed together in the van, pushed toward the entrance of Louisburg's heavily guarded harbor.

Anxious officers peering through their glasses from the decks of many ships were awed by what they saw. On either side of the harbor entrance were miniature forts, and from the ramparts of both protruded the muzzles of sixteen-pounder cannon. Behind them stood the great Citadel of Louisburg itself, a tribute to the ingenuity and cunning of the world's most talented military engineers. The walls that faced the harbor on one side and ran at right angles to it were sheer cliffs of stone, almost forty feet high. On the west, facing the town of Louisburg, and on the south, at the edge of a swampy plain, were slightly lower, star-shaped ramparts.

Oddly, the walls that faced due east, just south of the harbor entrance, were only twenty feet high. But there was a reason for this variation in Louisburg's architecture. Extending beyond the fort was a spit of land, approximately one mile long and half as wide, that was only a few feet above sea level. Apparently the builders of the fort had considered it indefensible, and had not included it within their walls. But they had foreseen that the eastern side of Louisburg might be particularly vulnerable to attack, and had built a number of artillery emplacements on the low ground, their guns facing seaward.

General Pepperrell immediately realized that this little spit of land might be the weak point in Louisburg's defenses. If the low ground could be captured, the powerful guns could be turned on the fort itself. He and Commodore Warren had worked out a system of rapid communications, and in a few moments a number of small, brightly colored pennants were run up to the topgallants of the *Massachusetts'* mainmast.

Sir Peter replied at once. He, too, had seen the relatively low walls and the artillery batteries beyond it, and the same thought had occurred to him. The military and naval commanders now had a specific objective.

The junior officers and enlisted men lining the rails of the troop transports began to doubt the wisdom of the campaign, and many wished they had gone home when they had been given the opportunity. Not in their wildest dreams had they imagined that Louisburg was so huge or so well-defended. The Citadel covered fifty-seven acres, and above the forty-foot walls towered ramparts of stone that soared another twenty feet. The shining brass muzzles of cannon jutted from openings everywhere.

The sentries on the musket platforms just behind the top edges of the parapets looked trim and efficient in their plumed, steel helmets and white uniforms edged with gold. And from the decks of the larger ships, it was possible to see the inner fort, a walled ring within a walled ring.

Suddenly Louisburg came alive. Trumpets blared, their sound floating across the water, and the men in the ships of the vanguard could hear the steady beating of drums. More soldiers appeared on the sentry platforms, gun crews hurried to their stations, and the elevation of cannon was changed. The banner of France, gold lilies on a field of white, was raised on a staff above the inner fort, and the elite of New France prepared to defend themselves.

As it happened, the Governor of Louisburg, Louis Dupont du Chambon, was eating his breakfast when the enemy was first sighted. A methodical man who had seen considerable service in the French navy, Admiral du Chambon had long been prepared for any emergency, and calmly finished his meal before going to the ramparts and inspecting the approaching fleet. He loathed grilled fish and filet of beef marinated in wine after they grew cold, and saw no reason to interrupt his breakfast. After all, every man in his command knew precisely how to deal with the situation.

In spite of their training, however, the defenders became slightly confused. They had rehearsed their invasion duties on many occasions, but this was the first time that an invader had actually appeared. Therefore they waited for an order from Admiral du Chambon before taking positive action.

So the approaching Englishmen and American colonials struck the first blows. Warren gave the initial honor to the *Massachusetts*, as a gesture to General Pepperrell. Captain Edward Tyng, a man who did not believe in wasting ammunition, personally directed his gunners, and his initial salvo of twelve-pounder shot peppered the batteries on the eastern lowlands.

Soon the cannon of all three Royal Navy frigates roared, as broadsides were aimed at the same batteries.

Then, in response to an order from Sir Peter, all of the British and American warships formed in a single line. Sailing past the low-lying ground, each directed its steady fire at the artillery batteries there. Meanwhile the transports anchored in the outer waters of Gabarus Bay, beyond the reach of Louisburg's mightiest cannon.

Admiral du Chambon was infuriated by his opponent's clever tactics. He had always assumed, as had both his predecessors and the engineers who had built the great fort, that any invader who came to Louisburg would try to force his way into the inner harbor, past the miniature forts that stood at either side of the half-mile-wide entrance.

But the calm of the sea made it possible for Commodore Warren to use an unorthodox technique. Instead of risking the terrible pounding his ships were sure to take if he tried to enter the inner harbor, he sailed back and forth as his gunners and those on the American ships silenced one battery after another on the eastern spit.

General Pepperrell had promised Colonel William Vaughan that, as the innovator of the plan to attack Louisburg, he would enjoy the privilege of being the first to land. The commander in chief was as good as his word, and after a two-hour bombardment of the eastern spit, sent a signal from the *Massachusetts* to the transports carrying the men of the First Regiment of Maine District Foot.

Sir Peter simultaneously created a diversion to distract the French. Detaching two of his fastest, most agile sloops of war from his battle line, he sent them closer to the towering sea wall of the fort directly south of the spot where the landing would take place. American militiamen stood on the decks of the transports watching as the two little sloops darted back and forth, defying guns whose shot could crush them.

The artillerymen manning the twenty-four-pounder cannon in the fort were professionals who knew their business, but they were at a disadvantage dealing with small, deft ships maneuvered by young Royal Navy captains whose seamanship was magnificent. The huge cannon roared, but the elusive sloops skipped beyond the reach of the heavy, red-hot iron balls that hurtled through the air. By the time each gun's elevation and range was changed, the sloops had darted elsewhere.

Admiral du Chambon watched the grim game, and that night made a notation in his daily journal. "The captains of the little English sloops drove me to distraction," he wrote. "My gunners were excellent, and did all that could be asked of them. But neither of the Englishmen was even grazed by a single shot. Some of my artillerymen believe the enemy possesses strange and magical powers that render our weapons impotent. I must crush the enemy quickly in order to disabuse them of the notion."

While the artillerymen manning the cannon in the sea wall were giving their full attention to the sloops, the British and American frigates inched closer to the low-lying spit of land and redoubled the fury of their bombardment. Warren was taking deliberate risks now, and paid for his audacity, as some of the guns on the shore were inflicting damage on his frigates. Cannoneers in the batteries beyond the low wall of Louisburg sent shot crashing into the hulls of the ships, cutting furrows in the planking of their decks and ripping several gaping holes in sails.

But there was a good reason for Warren's daring. A wind was blowing from east to west, and the thick clouds of smoke that his frigates' guns belched provided a perfect screen for a landing operation. The transports moved as close to the shore as they could, huddling under the protective bulk of the frigates, and lowered their longboats into the water.

Soldiers climbed down ladders into the boats, and the actual invasion began.

Colonel Vaughan raced a dozen of his men ashore, all of them jumping into knee-high water and wading toward dry land. Later accounts of the operation varied, but most agreed that the first man to climb onto the low-lying spit was a sergeant who had worked as a woodcutter in Kittery. This man, a husky giant named Phil Jones, had made a wager that he would be the first to win a French helmet as a prize, and was determined to make good his bet.

All accounts agreed that Colonel Vaughan was utterly fearless. He stood on the shore, indifferent to enemy fire, and waving his sword, directed his troops to fall into battle formation as they came up onto the land.

The French artillerymen discovered the ruse only after more than two hundred men had landed and were rushing toward the artillery batteries, which were protected by semicircular stone walls about eight feet high. These bulwarks would have served as good shields for infantry troops, but the artillerymen were not prepared for close combat.

A force of only eighty Frenchmen faced a full regiment of wilderness riflemen, the majority of whom were excellent shots. The odds against the defenders were overwhelming. A captain stationed at the lowest point behind the wall recognized the urgent need of his comrades, and sent help to them.

But, unfortunately for the artillerymen, there were only forty foot soldiers in the party that came to their aid. No reserve force was on duty inside the Citadel to repel such landings, since it had never occurred to the men who had built the fort or those who commanded it that an enemy might be able to gain a foothold anywhere in the vicinity. Therefore the forty infantrymen were the only troops available.

The Frenchmen fought with courage and determination. Crouching behind the semicircular stone walls that shielded the cannon, they used rifles and pistols to hold off the advancing enemy.

The Americans, exposed in the open, were completely unaccustomed to such opposition. But, as General Pepperrell later wrote to Governor Shirley, "They were too ignorant of their peril to shrink from their duty."

They threw themselves onto the muddy ground and crawled toward the French guns. Occasionally, when the white-uniformed troops eased their fire for a few moments in order to reload, the men from the Maine District leaped to their feet and raced forward a few, precious yards before pitching headlong into the mud again.

Their tactics bewildered the French, who had been taught a far more formal kind of warfare. In Europe, where they had been trained, armies formed in stiff ranks and fought their battles in what resembled a parade formation. The Americans, unfamiliar with European tactics and intent upon gaining their ends by any means, continued to push toward them.

Eventually the defenders were compelled to abandon their stronghold and retreat toward the fort. The men behind the walls of Louisburg were unable to offer them a protective cover of artillery fire to shield their withdrawal, and the victorious Americans moved into the artillery emplacements without further opposition.

The first to reach the site was Sergeant Phil Jones, who took the helmet of a dead enemy and waved it in triumph over his head. In later years the grim trophy would rest on the parlor mantel of his Kittery home.

Colonel Vaughan, advancing with the three majors who

were his battalion commanders, immediately realized the
enormous significance of the position he had attained. A
concerted rush on the miniature fort that stood at the
near side of the inner harbor entrance would make that
stronghold untenable for the enemy as well.

Reorganizing his troops, he left one battalion to hold
the artillery emplacements. These militiamen burrowed in
behind the heavy stone blocks to ward off the cannonading
from the Citadel that was certain to begin when the
French realized what was happening.

Vaughan, leading his other two battalions himself,
brandished his sword and started toward the little fort
known as the Grand Battery. His men spread out behind
him, instinctively employing the style used when fighting
Indians in the forest, in order to reduce the enemy's
target area.

The commander of the Grand Battery, Captain Chassin
de Thierry, was a professional soldier and a worthy
representative of an ancient, noble French family. He was
lacking in neither courage nor ingenuity, but realized,
with swiftly mounting horror, that he was helpless. His
powerful guns had been built for use against ships that
might try to sail through the narrow channel of the harbor
entrance, but were useless when employed against a thinly
spread line of individuals. His men needed muskets and
bayonets for that purpose, but had none.

There was only one thing he could do; with tears
streaming down his face, he ordered his cannoneers to
spike their guns. Long, heavy chunks of metal were
rammed down the barrels of the cannon, and then Captain de Thierry and his seventy-two men ran ignominiously
along the harbor edge to the Citadel, more than a mile
away.

The Maine District militiamen made no attempt to
stop them. Colonel Vaughan passed the word to his
battalion commanders that all efforts were to be con-

centrated on capturing the Grand Battery. The Americans obeyed, and poured into the miniature fort, which they found deserted. In fact, Captain de Thierry's men had been in such a hurry to depart that their spiking efforts had been slipshod, and Vaughan was pleased to discover that nine of the cannon could still be used.

Perhaps the most astonishing aspect of the Grand Battery's capture was that it was taken without the exchange of a single shot by the troops on either side. In later weeks, some of Captain de Thierry's superiors tried to make him a scapegoat, claiming that he had shown cowardice in battle. But Admiral du Chambon refused to support the charge, and so did the War Ministry when the matter was referred to Paris. There was nothing that De Thierry could have done to halt the advance of the Americans. And his troops had not had time to spike the cannon more effectively.

The accomplishments of the men from Maine within a brief span of two hours were stunning. First, they had gained a hold on the low-lying ground facing the weakest portion of the Citadel. And, thanks to the artillery emplacements there, it would be difficult for the mighty cannon of Louisburg to dislodge them.

Of far greater long-range significance was their capture of the Grand Battery. Americans now held one side of the harbor entrance, which would enable the fleet to enter more sheltered waters. A feat that the high command had hoped to accomplish in a week to ten days had been achieved in less than half of a single morning.

Seventeen French soldiers were killed in the engagement, and another twenty-four were wounded. But the men from Maine escaped almost unscathed. When the War Office in London eventually received a report on the operation, their lordships were incredulous. Only three Americans were wounded; one suffered no more than a slight scratch, and the other two endured injuries so slight that they returned to active service within a week.

Colonel Vaughan scribbled a brief note to General Pepperrell, and sent Sergeant Jones down to the shore to carry it out to the *Massachusetts* in one of the longboats. His message was long remembered throughout America: "May it please your Honor to be informed that by the grace of God and the courage of Maine men, I entered the Grand Battery about nine o'clock this morning. I am waiting for reinforcements and a flag."

General Waldo immediately came ashore with the rest of the Maine contingent, and strengthened the hold of the Americans on the ground they had taken.

Meanwhile Sir Peter was able to move his entire fleet closer to the Grand Battery, where the ships would be less vulnerable to attacks made by the Citadel's cannon. General Pepperrell also sent several crews of Rhode Islanders, his best cannoneers, to man the guns in the Grand Battery.

The largest guns of the Citadel opened a furious bombardment in an attempt to halt this activity, but most of the shots fell short by a considerable margin, as did those fired from the miniature fort on the far side of the harbor entrance, which was known as the Royal Battery.

The defenders were concentrating so hard on trying to keep the British and American colonial ships of war out of the harbor that General Pepperrell was able to achieve a master stroke. He sent transports carrying men from Massachusetts and Virginia to the south, and longboats carried them ashore onto the plain facing the towering, star-shaped walls of the Citadel.

Three regiments managed to land by mid-afternoon, and made a forced march across the swampy plain toward the southwest, until they reached a position out of reach of even the longest-range guns in Louisburg's armory. There they established their bivouac on a site that would, within a few days, become the main American camp.

This operation was accomplished without the loss of a single soldier. The only casualty was a mortified oarsman from Marblehead who was manning one of the longboats. He exerted too much effort when pulling on his oars, lost his balance, and tumbled overboard into the chilly waters of the Atlantic. His comrades hauled him out, and he was subsequently put to bed with a case of the ague, an ailment that, in a later day, would be called influenza.

By nightfall, General Pepperrell and Commodore Warren had good reason to feel that a near-miracle had been accomplished. Troops had established firm holds in two distinct sectors of Cape Breton Island. The men who occupied the land east of Louisburg commanded at least part of the harbor entrance, and were a severe threat to the security of the fort. Those on the swampy plain to the south were no more than a minor nuisance to the enemy at present, but were able to begin their siege.

Pepperrell and Warren went ashore together for a tour of inspection. First they visited the Grand Battery, which was the target of an incessant French bombardment. Few cannonballs struck the place, however, though the angry Admiral du Chambon repeatedly urged his gunners in the Citadel and the Royal Battery to drive the invaders out.

In order to make the position still more secure, regiments from Connecticut and New Hampshire were sent to join the men holding the Grand Battery. Now, if the French attempted an infantry sortie from the Citadel, the Americans would be able to hold their own.

General Pepperrell was also pleased by the landings on the plain, and ordered the troops from Massachusetts and Virginia to erect breastworks and dig trenches before putting up tents for their first night on the island. They, too, would be prepared if a party of foot soldiers came out of Louisburg in an effort to dislodge them.

Commodore Warren returned to the *Superbe* for the night, but General Pepperrell, ignoring the advice of his nervous aides, insisted on remaining ashore. He joined the militiamen from Massachusetts Bay; his tent was erected in the middle of their bivouac area, and his personal flag was raised above it. This pennant could be seen from the ramparts of the Citadel, and the gesture was intended as a direct, personal challenge to Admiral du Chambon.

Pepperrell wrote in his journal shortly after sundown: "I have dared my opposite number, the commander in chief of Louisburg, to drive me from his soil. He may, if he wishes, watch me dine on venison steak and cornmeal bread. Glasses are trained on me, as I write, from the turrets of Louisburg, and it would not surprise me to learn that Admiral du Chambon is himself observing me.

"Poor Du Chambon! He will not rest easily tonight. But I shall sleep soundly in the featherbed that is even now being carried across the plain for me after being landed from the *Massachusetts* from a whaleboat. How humiliating it must be for the commandant of the greatest fortress ever constructed by man to know we have achieved our initial landings so easily. How he must be grieving!

"But I do not gloat. I am thankful to the Almighty for that which we have already done, and I pray for His constant help in the long days ahead."

7

The first major task that faced the invaders of Louisburg, and it was urgent, was that of clearing the entrance to the inner harbor of all French obstructions. Only then could the naval vessels and transports move in and out with impunity.

So Commodore Warren decided to concentrate his complete attention on the reduction of the Royal Battery, which continued to guard the mouth of the narrow channel at the far side. A dawn conference of the high command was held on the second day of the invasion, and General Waldo, who was commanding the troops in possession of the eastern landspit, promised his full cooperation.

The nine guns of the Grand Battery that were still operable had already been trained on the twin miniature fort on the far side of the entrance, and at sunrise they began a heavy bombardment of the stronghold. At the same time the *Superbe,* the *Eltham,* and the *Mermaid* maneuvered into position for their own artillery attack.

The French, however, had not been inactive. Knowing the Royal Battery would be subjected to an assault, they had strengthened the bastion during the night. Additional gunners, supported by a full battalion of light infantrymen, had been sent there. And large quantities of gunpowder and shot had been moved there from the Citadel, along with supplies of food, water, and wine. The little fort, manned by more than five hundred veteran soldiers, was prepared to withstand a siege of its own.

The Rhode Islanders handling the captured cannon in the Grand Battery had never worked with such large guns, and found them unwieldy. They were so heavy and cumbersome that it was difficult to change their range. Crews of five men struggled together on each gun, raising or lowering its elevation. In spite of their size, these cannon proved unusually sensitive. Very slight changes in the charges of gunpowder caused the gunners to overshoot or undershoot their target. More than fifty rounds were fired before noon, and not once did the embarrassed Rhode Islanders hit their mark.

The French gunners in the Royal Battery suffered from no similar handicaps. Long accustomed to handling the huge guns, they subjected the miniature fort on the opposite side of the channel to a steady bombardment. Most of their shots bounced off the thick stones of the Grand Battery's walls without inflicting damage, but the Rhode Islanders, on the receiving end of artillery fire for the first time in their lives, became further distracted.

Then, at noon, a shot that was either lucky or a superb demonstration of marksmanship sailed through an open gunport. The heated ball glanced off the barrel of a cannon and landed on a pile of ammunition bags. The resulting explosion ripped a hole in the side of the little fort, killing eleven Rhode Islanders, including a lieutenant colonel, and wounded eight other men. The casualties were by far the worst the invaders had yet suffered.

Conditions in the miniature fort were so chaotic that it was impossible to resume firing for more than twenty-four hours. During that time, a number of stonemasons from several of the American regiments went to work repairing the damage. They had no cement, but managed to pile up enough stone blocks to make the wall relatively secure.

The French artillerymen, meanwhile, were able to devote their attention to the frigates of the British squadron. They worked coolly and efficiently, and actually gave better than they received. Scores of salvos were exchanged during the afternoon, and the French gunners scored three direct hits on the *Eltham*. None caused any significant damage, but Commodore Warren was forced to pay his adversaries greater respect, and drew off to a safer distance in order to fight a longer-range duel.

That night the French again carried large supplies of ammunition and powder from the Citadel to the Royal Battery under cover of darkness. By morning they were ready to resume the fight.

The frigate captains had received blistering reprimands from Sir Peter, and were still smarting from the tongue-lashing. Captain Ralph Lathrop of the *Superbe*, who subsequently became an admiral and enjoyed a brilliant career, wrote in his ship's log, "The Commodore summoned his Captains to a meeting, and called us fools, poltroons, and worse. He castigated us for gunnery far inferior to that of mere Frenchmen, and we, deserving his harsh words, vowed to do better when the battle for the Royal Battery is resumed."

Warren's anger made the captain and crew of the *Mermaid* a little too eager for combat. The frigate sailed almost within rifle range of the little fort to send a broadside of red-hot iron crashing down on the stone building. The aim of the Royal Navy gunners was exact, but the shots bounced off without causing any real damage.

The French, given an opportunity to retaliate in kind, seized their chance. One shot cracked the *Mermaid's* mainmast, which had to be replaced, another crashed through her stern, carrying away a portion of her fo'c'sle below decks, and a third killed five seamen on her main deck and wounded several others. She was forced to retire, and did not return to action for the better part of a week.

During this engagement, the Americans continued to send militiamen ashore from the transports, which were protected by the colonial warships. The camp on the plain south of Louisburg gradually became larger, and the infantry encountered no serious problems. Admiral du Chambon sent out none of his troops to attack them, but the huge twenty-four-pounder cannon emplaced behind forty-foot walls roared intermittently, reminding the invaders that the Citadel was far from ready to submit.

General Pepperrell realized that it would be impossible to reduce the great fortress without artillery, but the task of landing his guns seemed awesome. The shallows off the beach of the south shore were littered with huge boulders which made it hazardous to maneuver longboats and other small craft bringing men ashore. These rocks proved an even greater obstacle to the landing of cumbersome cannon.

Two boats, unable to ride through the surf, crashed into boulders. A number of men were drowned in the accidents, and both cannon were lost.

But there was no other way to bring the artillery ashore. Marblehead fishermen, long accustomed to operating in rock-strewn surf, enjoyed the greatest success, and eventually were given the entire chore. These militiamen worked ceaselessly for the better part of a week, and although they suffered many further casualties, they finally completed their assignment.

Thirty-four cannon, including six howitzers, at last stood on wheeled platforms near the beach, their ammunition and shot secure from the elements under tarpaulins. "Never," Captain Jebediah Martin of Marblehead wrote to his wife, "have I known such hard work. I wonder how we did it, and I marvel that I have lived to write you these few words."

In all, twenty-three men had died in the operation, seventeen others had suffered serious injuries, and four cannon had been lost. The boats carrying these guns had been smashed beyond repair. But all of the remaining artillery was on shore, as was the rest of Pepperrell's army. He was ready now to move against Louisburg.

No concerted attack could be made against the fort, however, until the Royal Battery was reduced, and at the end of a full week, Commodore Warren's warships had still not attained this objective. The sloops tried to divert the attention of the French gunners, but failed to fool seasoned veterans. And when Captain Tyng of the *Massachusetts* received permission to try his luck against the sturdy little bastion, he quickly discovered that his gunners were no match for the enemy, and discreetly withdrew from the contest.

Admiral du Chambon knew precisely what was happening in the enemy camp, of course, because the Americans and Englishmen were under constant observation from the turrets of the sixty-foot-high defense towers that loomed above Louisburg. Therefore it was not a whim or mere chance that dictated the timing of the first French cavalry assault.

The American infantry, after spending a full week in bivouac, was becoming bored, and a trifle careless. One afternoon, when heavy rain clouds darkened the sky, the duel between the warships and the Royal Battery was postponed until the weather improved. The militiamen retired to their tents, leaving only their sentries in the open. Lightning flashed off to the west, thunder rumbled, and the first warning drops of light rain began to fall.

Suddenly one of Louisburg's south gates opened, and four squadrons of cavalry, approximately three hundred men in all, rode out at a gallop and swept across the plain in perfect formation, heading toward the American bivouac. In the lead was Colonel Adrien de Joinville, Comte d'Amboise, a distinguished cavalryman with a long record of combat success in France's minor wars of the past quarter century. Accompanying him were some of the world's finest horsemen, eager to demonstrate their skill.

Too late, the sentries, members of a Massachusetts Bay battalion, gave the warning. Before men could snatch their rifles and muskets, run out into the open and form defense lines, the French squadrons were upon them.

Wielding their sabers magnificently, the riders slashed through the camp of three regiments, cutting down individual militiamen who tried to oppose them, knocking down tents, and creating havoc. Then, before the stunned Americans could recover, the horsemen galloped back to the Citadel, still riding in straight, evenly spaced lines.

They disappeared and the gates shut behind them just as the rainstorm broke.

The Americans were left to tend their wounded and bury their dead. They salvaged what they could of smashed supply boxes, and put up their crumpled tents. The sortie had lasted no more than a quarter of an hour, and in that time the French had done almost incalculable damage to the bivouacs of regiments from New York, Pennsylvania, and New Hampshire.

"Tonight," General Pepperrell ruefully noted in his journal, "it is the turn of Admiral du Chambon to sleep soundly."

The Englishmen and Americans desperately needed some token to lift their spirits. After their initial, easy successes, the invasion had bogged down in a morass of failures and irritations. Nothing was going well, and the French were still secure behind the walls of their fortress.

Commodore Warren's primary objective remained that of reducing the Royal Battery, which barred the warships and transports of the invasion fleet from the secure waters of the inner harbor. So far, he knew, he had been fortunate. Only one rainstorm had blown up, and the seas had remained calm. But spring was an unpredictable season off Cape Breton Island, and he realized that, sooner or later, high winds and wild seas might scatter his ships over a wide area.

General Pepperrell had a new but equally pressing concern. A French courier, who knew nothing about the arrival of the invasion fleet, arrived at Louisburg from Quebec on board a small sloop, which was captured by the *Connecticut*. The courier was made prisoner, and his letter to Admiral du Chambon was given to General Pepperrell.

Its contents were alarming. A full regiment of Regulars was already traveling from Quebec to reinforce the garrison, and was accompanied by a group referred to only as "the good Abbé and his friends."

Pepperrell knew at once whom the French meant, and so did every one of the officers he called to an emergency council of war. A French missionary, Abbé Jean Louis le Loutre, had spent a number of years living among the Micmac, one of the most savage of all the Indian tribes in New France. It appeared that he and an unspecified number of warriors were also marching toward Louisburg.

France, Pepperrell knew, had adapted far better to New World conditions than any other European nation. Although some of her regimental and battalion commanders still fought in the hollow, square formations that had been in military vogue since the time of the Roman legions, others had learned to go into battle Indian style. That meant they used trees, boulders, and heavy underbrush as cover, spreading out as they went into combat. It was possible, even probable, that a regiment making the long march toward Cape Breton Island from Quebec would employ the New World techniques that made it more formidable and reduced casualties.

If so, two or three regiments of the untried American militiamen would have to oppose them in order to equalize the odds. The numerical advantage that General Pepperrell enjoyed would be materially reduced.

In the event that Abbé le Loutre and the Micmac also

landed on the island, the Americans' problems would be further compounded. The savages undoubtedly would be equipped with French muskets, and the American high command would be forced to send its most experienced frontiersmen against them. As a result, the potency of Pepperrell's corps would be dissipated. Worse still, his forces would be caught between the new regiment of French Regulars and the Micmac on one side and the powerful Louisburg garrison on the other. Between them, they could squeeze him in a pincers movement until they compelled him to abandon his attack.

It was therefore imperative that the commander in chief step up the pace of his attack on the fort before Admiral du Chambon received reinforcements. Every day's gains were important, and it was small consolation that the defenders of Louisburg, cut off from the outside world, did not know that help was on the way.

The infantry could do nothing unless it received strong support from the artillery, so it was obvious that the Rhode Island guns had to be moved forward, within range of the fort. General Pepperrell gave the order to Colonel Thomas W. Hanscomb, the Rhode Island commander, and then went with him to watch the operation.

From the outset, the attempt was a nightmare. The cannon were so heavy that they sank into the swampy ground. Infantrymen were summoned to help, but no sooner was a gun hauled out of the mud than it sank again. The senior officers, watching the French on the ramparts of the Citadel, saw the enemy laughing at them.

Finally, after great efforts had been expended in vain over a period of several days, Colonel Nathaniel Meserve of New Hampshire had an idea that, he believed, might solve the problem. "I suggest," he said in a memorandum to General Pepperrell, "that your Honor try using stone boats to move the guns."

"I was chagrined," the commander in chief later wrote

in his journal, "that the same thought had not occurred to me."

Every New Englander who had ever cleared his fields of large rocks, and had subsequently used the stones he had collected to erect a fence or build a house, was familiar with such "boats." They were actually barges used on land, flat platforms of wood, hauled by oxen and piled high with stones.

Stone boats larger and sturdier than those used for hauling away rocks were needed for pulling cannon. Woodsmen went off to the forest southwest of the Citadel, adjacent to the swampy plain, and cut down the biggest evergreens they could find. Men who had been carpenters in civilian life made them into planks. Then, under Colonel Meserve's direction, barges or platforms sixteen feet long and five feet wide were constructed.

No oxen were available, of course, and the horses of the few cavalry squadrons were too high-spirited to be worked in unison as dray animals. Manpower was the only answer to this newest problem, and General Pepperrell asked for volunteers. More than one thousand men responded, and most of them were needed. In all, six of the special stone boats were made. They were so heavy after being loaded with cannon that teams of one hundred men were required to haul each of them.

The ingenious device was effective, and the troops, straining hard, pulled the guns forward. Once they came within range of the Citadel's guns, however, a new complication developed. The French opened a blistering cannon fire of their own, forcing the Americans to abandon their efforts. Again Pepperrell and his senior commanders were dismayed.

Several more days passed before they found ways to counter the French move. Parties armed with shovels and picks were sent forward at night to dig and erect breastworks. This was a relatively simple task, as the ground was spongy, and the defenders in the Citadel could not see what was taking place. The earthworks the troops built were reinforced with short sections of logs, and each makeshift shield was constructed in semicircular form, its outer side facing Louisburg.

These shields afforded only a partial protection from the fort's powerful guns, but most cannonballs bounced off them, and only a direct, pinpointed strike could cut through the thick walls of earth and wood. At last the Rhode Island guns could be moved forward, and this task was also accomplished under cover of darkness.

Thereafter, for the duration of the siege, French and American cannon dueled incessantly from daybreak until sunset each day. "We expend iron at such a rapid rate," Colonel Hanscomb wrote in his military diary, "that we would run short of ammunition were we not obliged by the enemy, who fires at us, at the same furious rate. Some French shot fit our cannon. Most are too large, but we have found a method of reducing them. Ironsmiths from Massachusetts Bay and Pennsylvania have built a huge fire near the beach, and using it night and day, fashion the shot to fit our own cannon."

The siege was beginning to show progress. Although no one knew how much damage was being inflicted on the enemy, it was reasonable to assume that cannonballs soaring over the parapets of the Citadel were smashing rooftops and otherwise making life uncomfortable for the defenders of Louisburg.

However the Royal Battery still held out, and the marksmanship of its gunners continued to deny the inner harbor to Sir Peter Warren's fleet. The invaders knew they could not hope to reduce the fort until they took possession of the harbor. And the fear still persisted that the fleet might be scattered by a severe storm.

The difficulty was fundamental, as Commodore Warren noted in his log. "My fire power is insufficient to silence the cannon of the Royal Battery," he wrote. "I am convinced I need a ship of the line for the purpose."

Yet no matter how great the need, he and his subordinates realized that the Admiralty in London had no intention of sending the squadron one of the monarchs of the sea.

Early one afternoon, however, a ship was seen in the distance, approaching Louisburg, and when she drew somewhat nearer it was obvious that she was no merchantman. Sir Peter ordered his warships to strip for action, and they immediately prepared to do battle with the intruder.

After another anxious half hour, the strange vessel hoisted her flag to her mains'l topgallants, and the English and American seamen cheered when they saw the British flag. The newcomer, it developed, was another Royal Navy frigate, the *Launceton,* of forty-four guns, which the Admiralty had sent from European waters.

She joined in the attack on the Royal Battery the following day, and the bombardment of the French bastion was heavier than it had been at any time since the beginning of the siege. But the French continued to hold out. "The *Launceton* is a welcome addition," Sir Peter wrote in his log, "but she cannot strike the French banner from its mast, nor can any frigate. The range of her cannon is too short, and if she sails close to the shore, the batteries there would smash her to kindling."

The invaders' warships maintained their futile, exasperating patrol for day after weary day. Then, at noon one day, about two weeks after the siege began, a sloop of war from Connecticut that had been ranging far to sea as a "watchdog" raced toward Louisburg under full sail. A huge French ship of the line was sailing toward Cape Breton Island, her captain told Sir Peter, and would appear later in the day.

Commodore Warren commanded four English and two American frigates, as well as a large number of smaller vessels. But his biggest cannon were eighteen-pounders, with a range far shorter than that of a ship of the line's giant twenty-four-pounders. The one enemy man-of-war was capable of blowing his ships out of the water before a single English or American vessel could land a shot.

Sir Peter realized that his only chance lay in deception. If the enemy ship of the line had not yet learned that Louisburg was under siege, he might be able to lure her close enough to make effective use of his guns.

His entire squadron put out to sea immediately. It was essential, he knew, to meet the enemy ship sufficiently far from Louisburg to prevent the guns of the Citadel and the Royal Battery from warning her of his identity.

For the better part of two hours the squadron sailed toward the east, aided by a brisk wind. Sir Peter put his ships into the formation ordinarily used by the French, who believed in massed fire power, and had little use for sloops, schooners, and other small vessels. The frigates sailed in the van, in pairs, with the *Superbe* and the *Launceton* leading the procession. The sloops and schooners fanned out innocently on the flanks, and Sir Peter hoped that the enemy captain would think his squadron was French.

At last a cry from the lookout in the flagship warned that the ship of the line was on the horizon. She and the squadron moved closer, and a Royal Navy lieutenant, who climbed high into the rigging of the *Superbe,* identified the French ship as the *Vigilant,* a monster armed with seventy-four guns, most of them devastating twenty-four-pounders.

The British and American ships were warned not to show their colors until the flagship set the example. Meanwhile the entire squadron quietly prepared for battle. Cooking fires were extinguished, and buckets of sand were placed at intervals on all decks for the purpose of putting out fires caused by the French warship. Gun crews were ordered to their stations, but ports were not lowered, since the appearance of cannon would be a certain indication to the man-of-war that the squadron was hostile.

Anxious officers on the quarterdecks, sailing crews gathered on the main decks, and gun crews crouching beside their weapons waited in an atmosphere of swiftly mounting tension. The strain was particularly difficult for the gunnery officers and their men. With gunports closed they could see nothing, and in the event the man-of-war opened fire, the first they might know of the attack would be the crashing of red-hot iron balls through the ports. Men could die without even realizing they had been hit.

The *Vigilant* maintained her course toward Louisburg, and her captain apparently did not think it odd that the squadron was heading straight toward her. This was not surprising, since friendly ships often sailed close enough to each other to exchange messages. The range grew shorter.

Finally, however, the captain of the French warship became suspicious. He had not been told by his superiors in Paris that a French squadron of such size was operating in North Atlantic waters, and he decided to find out whether the strange ships were friendly or hostile. While still somewhat beyond the range of the frigate's guns, he ran up his colors.

The courtesies of the sea, regardless of nationality, called for a reply. But Commodore Warren took his time, since each passing moment worked to his advantage. Well aware that he was being observed from the enemy's quarterdeck, he instructed the captain of the *Superbe* to pretend his lines were fouled. The young officer in charge of the operation put on a fine show in pantomime, energetically berating the two sailors whose job it was to run up flags from the base of the mainmast. The squadron continued to edge closer.

Commodore Warren's words, breaking the silence, were to become legendary in both England and her North

American colonies. "The day is rather cool," he said calmly, "and I believe we need a bit of exercise to warm our blood. Captain, show your colors! Flag Lieutenant, be good enough to make a signal to my squadron. Order all ships to strip for action and move into battle formation."

Signal flags were hoisted with the Union Jack, and the tiny squares of colored cloth whipped in the breeze.

The other ships of the squadron immediately broke out their distinguishing pennants, too. Simultaneously they split into two columns, each moving in single file. Heading to port were the *Superbe*, the *Eltham*, and the *Massachusetts*, with the *Launceton*, the *Mermaid*, and the *Connecticut* moving to starboard. The sloops and schooners of the squadron closed in, taking their own places in the lines, which began to resemble two scythes enveloping the enemy.

Gunports were lowered, and the squadron was ready for action.

At last the captain of the *Vigilant* realized he was being trapped, and tacked sharply, hoping to escape. But a ship of the line, because of its size and weight, could not maneuver with the swift grace of frigates or of still smaller ships. Quickly discovering that he could not sail out of danger, the Frenchman decided to blast his way out. He, too, began to strip for action.

By this time, however, the enemy was upon him. Sir Peter gave the order to open fire, and as each of the frigates on either side of the *Vigilant* sailed even with her, it raked her with a broadside. Then, while the six frigates turned about to repeat the operation from the opposite direction, the agile little sloops darted in, followed by the somewhat slower schooners, to pepper the massive French warship with their nine-pounders. This small shot bounced harmlessly off the *Vigilant*'s thick hull, but the sloops and schooners managed to distract the suddenly alarmed French crew, and thereby accomplished their purpose.

Again the guns of the six frigates roared, and ten to fifteen shots ripped through the *Vigilant*'s rigging, crashed onto her decks and split the beams of her hull. Thanks to long practice, Royal Navy gunners were able to fire three salvos while in position, and on the second and third rounds their marksmanship improved. The gunners on the *Massachusetts* and *Connecticut* had known few of the benefits of rigorous training, but they fired two salvos before sailing out of range, and although their weapons were inferior, they scored a number of strikes.

"It was the privilege of the *Massachusetts*," Captain Tyng wrote Governor Shirley, "to inflict two severe blows on the French ship. One of our shots damaged her quarter-deck, and the other sheared off a portion of her rudder."

Then the mammoth guns of the *Vigilant* roared. Seagulls following the squadron from Cape Breton Island, although not frightened by the sounds of lesser cannon, now wheeled in the air and headed back toward the land, their wings flapping wildly. The French gunners overshot their targets, which was precisely what Commodore Warren had hoped. Twenty-four-pounders were too powerful to be effective at close range unless their trajectory were lowered drastically, and while the French gunnery officers worked to improve their aim, Warren had the opportunity to tack and return to the battle.

At least four of his frigates found the range at the same time; according to some accounts, five of the six hit the target. Part of the *Vigilant*'s main deck was splintered and, more important, her mainmast was shot away in several places. Only the rigging held up the separated fragments.

The ship of the line was helpless now, and her captain, recognizing his inability to continue the fight, struck his colors. Commodore Warren at once ordered the squadron to cease its operations. His gig was lowered, and, accompanied by his staff, he was rowed to the French ship, where he accepted the sword of her captain. The French commander, his officers, and men were made prisoners, and the *Vigilant* was seized as a prize of war.

A British skeleton crew went aboard to sail her back to Cape Breton Island, a feat that was accomplished with great difficulty because she was crippled. But Commodore Warren knew she would be seaworthy again after his carpenters put in a few days of making repairs.

Warren's victory was a significant episode in the siege. He had acquired as a flagship a man-of-war whose guns were capable of pounding the Royal Battery from a safe distance. The prospects of the campaign had become immeasurably brighter.

8

The duel between the British gunners on board the captured man-of-war and the French artillerymen in the Royal Battery at the entrance to the Louisburg harbor was so intense that General Pepperrell wrote in his journal, "All of us are deafened by the unceasing roar of the cannon. If there be hell on earth, accompanied by fire, smoke, and destruction, we are experiencing it."

So many shots fired by the warship plowed into the ground in the vicinity of the Royal Battery that Cape Breton Island fishermen were still digging them up as souvenirs more than one hundred years after the battle. The British enjoyed the natural advantage in the duel: the Royal Battery remained in the same place, but the *Vigilant* shifted her position frequently, making her an elusive target.

"I marvel at the tenacious courage of the French gunners who remain at their posts," Parson Moody wrote to his wife. "Those who survive the terrible ordeal deserve the highest rewards their King & Country can bestow upon them. But, alas! There will be few who can live after tolerating such a drubbing. I pray for their souls."

Both sides knew the issue was climactic, and used gunpowder and shot recklessly. The *Vigilant's* cannon became so overheated there was a constant danger that one or more might explode. So buckets of sea water were poured over the barrels at regular intervals. The din was almost too great to be endured, and, according to Commodore

Warren's records, the hearing of at least five gunners was permanently impaired.

The French suffered far worse than did their adversaries. Not only did the French artillerymen have to stand at their posts all day—every day—in the miniature fort, but they also had to remain alert every night for a possible surprise landing by American infantry. Members of the garrison became gaunt skeletons. A sergeant named Emile Joseph Gautier, who weighed more than two hundred pounds when the siege began, was reduced to one hundred and twenty-five pounds when it ended.

There was one advantage the French continued to enjoy, however. The British and American colonials had brought their shot and powder with them, and hence their supplies were limited. But huge quantities of munitions were still stored in the Citadel's stone cellars. The French could better afford to be prodigal.

As the days passed, the strain began to tell on the invaders, although Sir Peter was determined not to slacken the pace of his attack. Sooner or later, he felt certain, the enemy would be compelled to give up the Royal Battery. Meanwhile, more shot and powder were needed, and the *Mermaid*, which could sail more rapidly than any of the other frigates, was sent off to Boston. Her captain carried a message from General Pepperrell to Governor Shirley.

"The Commodore and I find we expend iron at a faster rate than we anticipated," the commander in chief of the land force wrote. "Our resolution has not wavered, but, if we are to accomplish our goal, we must become beggars. We plead with Your Excellency to fill the hold of the *Mermaid* with as much coarse-grained powder and twenty-four-pounder shot as she will carry, and return her to us with all due speed. If we are deprived of the sinews of war, all is lost. If Your Excellency can fill our needs, we shall return home victorious."

Pepperrell realized that both iron and gunpowder were

1   Portrait of William Pitt, First Earl of Chatham, by the studio of R. Brompton.   *Courtesy of the National Portrait Gallery, London.*

2   View of the landing of New England forces in the expedition against Cape Breton Island, by J. Stevens.   Courtesy of the Mabel Brady Garvan Collection, Yale University Art Gallery.

3 General William Pepperrell at the siege of Louisburg. *Courtesy of the Bettmann Archive.*

4   Portrait of General William Pepperrell by John Smibert.   *Courtesy of the Essex Institute, Salem, Massachusetts.*

scarce everywhere in the colonies. But he also knew that Shirley was a resourceful man who would do everything in his power to obtain the required ammunition.

William Shirley lived up to his friend's expectations. The supplies of coarse-grained powder stored in the Boston arsenal on Beacon Hill, near Thomas Hancock's new mansion, were reserved for the use of the militia battalions on duty in the western part of the colony. If he took them, the wilderness settlements would be unable to defend themselves. Shirley unhesitatingly gambled. It was better to use the stocks on hand in the hope that a victory over Louisburg would make the western frontiers secure, he reasoned. Willingly jeopardizing his reputation and the future of Massachusetts Bay, he took the gunpowder, explaining his actions in a report to the Colonial Office in London.

There was literally no shot for twenty-four-pounder cannon in Boston, or, for that matter, elsewhere in New England. Undaunted, Shirley appealed to the citizens for help, and the people of Boston responded without delay. Wealthy home owners ripped out fences and gates of wrought iron, housewives contributed precious skillets and kettles that were made only in England and hence were difficult to replace. Stonemasons worked around the clock to build a huge hearth at one end of a waterfront warehouse, and the iron was melted there, then fashioned into shot.

Within a scant seventy-two hours of her arrival in Boston the *Mermaid* started back to Cape Breton Island. Her hold was so crammed with munitions that she rode low in the water, but she traveled under full sail at the fastest speed she could maintain.

She rejoined the invaders on May 23, and Commodore Warren celebrated her arrival by subjecting the Royal Battery to a furious new bombardment. So much shot was fired within the span of a single hour that the principal gunnery officer on board the *Vigilant* was unable to estimate how much he had used.

Battered and discouraged, the French artillerymen in the miniature fort could hold out no longer. They had been heartened by the slackening of enemy fire during the *Mermaid*'s absence from Cape Breton Island, but the renewed fury of the attack broke their spirit. Their lily pennant was hauled down, and a flag of surrender was raised in its place.

Commodore Warren, who had been observing the bombardment from the Great Battery, immediately set out by boat for the little fort, accompanied by General Waldo. Scores of Maine militiamen followed in whaleboats, and couriers were sent to the plain south of the Citadel to tell General Pepperrell the good news.

The defenders of the Royal Battery had fought so gallantly that Sir Peter Warren granted them generous surrender terms. All officers were permitted to keep their swords and pistols, and every Frenchman who had taken part in the fight was granted a free choice. Those who wished could march unhindered to the Citadel, but those who were sick of the war could remain with the invaders under lenient prisoner of war conditions. Without exception the French elected to join their comrades in the Citadel.

They marched off down the harbor road to the main fort, while the American militiamen saluted them by standing at attention until they had gone. Then the British flag was hoisted, and the troops were sent out to collect as much twenty-four-pounder shot, fired by the *Vigilant*, as they could retrieve from the surrounding area.

At long last the entrance to the inner harbor was completely under Commodore Warren's control. The sloops and schooners remained in the open sea on patrol duty, but the rest of the fleet, warships and transports alike, sailed into the harbor. All of the vessels stayed close to the mouth, however, maintaining as great a distance as they could from the huge guns of the Citadel.

The French artillerymen who had surrendered the Royal Battery had not spiked any of the little fort's guns. Perhaps the final bombardment had dazed them, perhaps they had been observing the strict code of surrender, under which it was considered a criminal act to render weapons inoperable.

Whatever their reason, the British and American colonials now had six twenty-four-pounder cannon in perfect condition. General Pepperrell arrived to confer with Commodore Warren, and they finally decided to leave three of the big guns in the Royal Battery. The other three would be moved to the plain south of Louisburg, where they would back up the Rhode Islanders' far smaller guns.

Transporting the cannon proved to be a task that taxed the patience of the invaders to the breaking point. Commodore Warren chose the *Eltham*, the smallest of the British frigates, as the carrier. Her crew and more than three hundred militiamen labored for a full day to hoist the heavy guns onto her main deck. One of the cannon slipped from the ropes holding its muzzle, and crashed onto the deck of the *Eltham* with such force that more than forty feet of planking subsequently had to be replaced.

Then the *Eltham* sailed off to the south beach, and the following day the cannon were carried ashore, one by one. Three men were killed and six others injured in the difficult, delicate operation, and a longboat was smashed. New barges had been made to haul the big guns across swampy ground, but the first cannon to be hoisted onto a platform sank more than four feet into the mud.

Colonel Hanscomb, the Rhode Island artillery commander, promptly took off his uniform coat and waded into the slime. He was followed by no less a personage than General Pepperrell, who did not bother to remove his gold-braided coat, and who showed no concern for his finery. The militiamen were astonished by the sight, and, cheering loudly, raced forward into the swamp by the hundreds.

After a short, hard struggle, the big gun was hauled out of the mud and pulled back onto firmer ground. Everyone was filthy, and no man looked more disreputable than General Pepperrell. His scarlet tunic and white breeches were smeared with mud, dirt was caked on his high boots, and even his gold epaulets, the symbol of his rank, were mud-stained.

But this one simple act of sharing the discomfort of his men won him the affection of the entire corps. Thereafter, the troops were willing to suffer any hardship he demanded, and he achieved a popularity that no other American would attain until the American Revolution, three decades later, when General George Washington would inspire similar loyalty.

In spite of Pepperrell's gesture, however, the problem of how to handle twenty-four-pounder cannon on swampy ground remained unsolved. A number of officers conferred at length, and this time it was Colonel Hanscomb who found the answers.

First, he said, emplacement sites should be prepared, and scores of men carried heavy rocks and logs to the places he designated. These would provide firm bedding for the cannon. Then he had the carpenters make triple runners, each of them twenty-five feet long, which were attached to the undersides of the stone boats or barges. Resembling the runners on children's sleds, the strips of wood helped to distribute the weight of the cannon more evenly.

Finally, a whole battalion of troops was sent out into the woods to the west, where the men collected large quantities of small, red berries, which had proved inedible. After being boiled, the berries turned into a thick paste, which was applied to the runners. When the substance hardened it formed a heavy, exceptionally slick wax that made it relatively easy to haul one of the barges across the soft, spongy ground.

An experiment with a single stone boat proved successful, so troops were assigned the task of preparing the emplacements. The French, however, knew precisely what the enemy was doing, and why, and their own twenty-four-pounder cannon laid down a heavy barrage. They realized the necessity of preventing the Americans from establishing sites for long-range guns capable of battering the walls of the Citadel, and did all they could to hamper the operation.

The bombardment was too heavy for the gun beds to be prepared during daylight hours, so following the same procedure that had been used with success when the smaller cannon had been moved forward, the work crews waited until night to begin their labors.

But the French were now prepared to counter such operations, and on the first night the attempt was made, cavalry squadrons were sent out to harass the Americans. The following night Colonel Hanscomb tried again, and this time the work crews were protected by a battalion of Virginia marksmen and a full regiment from New York.

Again the French rode out of the Citadel, and a sharp skirmish, the first of the campaign, took place. The confusion of fighting at night caused heavy casualties on both sides, and both drew back. The French were the real victors in the engagement, however, because they stopped the work crews from preparing the bedding for the captured twenty-four-pounder guns.

On the third night, both sides increased the size of their forces. The Americans sent out three full regiments to screen the work crews, and a full regiment of French light infantry supported the attacking cavalry squadrons. Again there were casualties as men milled about in the dark.

But General Pepperrell ordered the men assigned to the bedding task to perform their labors regardless of the fighting swirling around them. They obeyed, working with such vigor that they completed the better part of their assignment before the entire American force pulled back.

On the fourth night, during still another skirmish, work on the bedding was finished. But General Pepperrell, aware that many more days would pass before the guns could be moved into position if the present rate of progress were not improved, directed that protective shields be erected for the cannon during the day, no matter how hard the artillery of Louisburg tried to disrupt this final phase of preparations. He knew that the regiment from Quebec and the Micmac could appear at any time, so the opportunities of each passing day were precious.

Troops from Massachusetts Bay, Connecticut, and Pennsylvania volunteered, and went out to brave the enemy fire. The batteries of twenty-four-pounders in the Citadel roared all day, occasionally driving back the militiamen for short periods. But the Americans returned to their task each time, and by nightfall they had prepared semicircular breastworks of earth, reinforced with logs and stones.

Colonel Hanscomb's "sleds" proved to be so effective that all of the big cannon were moved into place within two hours early that evening, before the French made their expected sortie. Quantities of powder and ammunition were brought forward. Then all three guns fired a salvo as a way of notifying the French that, in spite of the harassment, the cannon were operable. Not until the next day was it ascertained that two of the shots probably had fallen short, and that only one had struck the towering wall of the Citadel.

The relative ineffectiveness of the salvo was unimportant. The French had been warned that, at least to an extent, the odds had been equalized. On the same night Admiral du Chambon wrote a letter to the authorities at

Quebec, saying, "My own twenty-four-pounders have been turned against me. I need assistance. Send me cavalry, infantry, and such Indian warriors as can be relied upon. The English-speaking colonials are as persistent as swamp flies."

A messenger carrying the letter was captured by sentries from New Jersey, and the letter was taken to General Pepperrell. What no one in the British-American colonial high command realized, however, was that the besieged governor of Louisburg had actually dispatched three couriers, hoping that at least one of them would be able to make his way to Quebec. Not until much later was it learned that two of the messengers had reached their destination.

For the immediate present, General Pepperrell's chief concern was the protection of his artillery. Now that he had acquired several of the large cannon, he was afraid the enemy would make a determined effort to render all of his guns inoperable. Therefore four regiments were assigned to stand guard over the emplacements, two of them stationed near the twenty-four-pounders and the other two at the sites of the smaller guns.

Admiral du Chambon was indeed tempted to try to put the American cannon out of commission. But his attempts to prevent the emplacement of the twenty-four-pounders had been a costly failure. He had lost fifty men killed and wounded in the unsuccessful sorties, and his garrison was already too small to risk the additional sapping of vitally needed manpower.

Had he been able to send out skirmishing parties in strength it might have been possible for him to scatter the inexperienced American colonials and, perhaps, force them to withdraw from Cape Breton Island. But he was suffering from a severe handicap, and could only sit behind his walls in angry frustration, hoping that sooner or later help would reach him.

9

In theory, the invaders had good reason to feel satisfied with their progress. They had gained control of the entrance to the inner harbor of Louisburg, and had established emplacements of artillery on the plain south of the fort. It would not be easy to dislodge them, and if they could maintain their pressure long enough, they would force the enemy to surrender.

In practice, however, life was becoming increasingly difficult. No member of the expedition had been prepared for the conditions that made day-to-day existence on Cape Breton Island harsh and uncompromising beyond belief. Illness, not the French, was the worst enemy the invaders had to fight.

Sailors and soldiers alike depended almost completely on the supplies of food they had brought with them from the colonies. The only exception was fresh fish, which seamen from the sloops, schooners, and some of the smaller transports caught daily. For a time the more enterprising sailors sold their catches to anyone who could pay their prices, but, as belts tightened, Commodore Warren sent out official fishing parties.

Much of the invaders' stores of corn and wheat was rotten, and had to be discarded. Sack after sack was thrown away, and General Pepperrell was forced to issue an order forbidding the men to dump the spoiled grains into the sea for fear of polluting the waters. Preserved beef and pork was sometimes inedible, and the members of a battalion from New Hampshire became violently ill after eating the contents of several barrels of pickled pork.

Feelings against the contractors who had sold foodstuffs to the militia regiments ran high, and the troops spoke in terms of lynching the men who had made a profit at their expense. Only a few, among them Thomas Hancock, had been completely honest in their dealings with the supply masters of the corps, and had sold them untainted provisions.

The ships of the Royal Navy squadron were somewhat more fortunate. There were always British warships in the New World, and the Admiralty was a steady customer, so the men who sold food to Commodore Warren's supply master had been more careful. The quality of the beef and pork the sailors ate was inferior, to be sure, but the meat was not spoiled.

The militiamen went on half rations only three weeks after landing on Cape Breton Island, far sooner than General Pepperrell or General Waldo had anticipated. Contrary to the original expectations of the supply masters, it was not possible to buy additional provisions in the town of Louisburg, which lay due west of the fort, nestling in its shadow.

The artillery of the Citadel formed a blanket which protected the town and made it impossible for British or American purchasing agents to visit the shopkeepers. Some of the troops grumbled, but General Pepperrell was content to include the little town in the siege. It was strictly against all rules of eighteenth-century warfare to campaign actively against civilians. But it was fair enough to prevent the residents of Louisburg from going outside their town limits.

These unfortunate people, cut off from the farms of the hinterland and from the mainland of New France, were forced to depend on Admiral du Chambon for their own food supplies. It was Pepperrell's hope that they would prove a burden on the Governor, and would drain the fort's reserves of food.

Only a few troops, most of them from Connecticut and New Jersey, were stationed west of the town to prevent the people from buying fresh meat, eggs, and vegetables from the farmers whose property stretched out for a distance of about thirty miles of cultivated land. The citizens of Louisburg proved remarkably docile, and the militiamen rarely were forced to turn back anyone who wanted to go beyond the lines that General Pepperrell had established in the sector. For a time this meekness had been puzzling to men accustomed to the aggressiveness displayed by others who earned their living on the raw wilderness frontiers of the New World.

The troops soon learned the reason for it. When the supply masters of the corps went to the farmers of Cape Breton Island to obtain provisions, they found that the overwhelming majority of property owners were very poor. Most were unable to earn a living from the rocky soil for themselves and their families, and were receiving financial assistance from the French government.

The men who had planned and built Louisburg had hoped that, after some decades, the entire island would become a self-sufficient fortress; that the farmers would grow enough food to sustain the Citadel's garrison and the residents of the little town serving it. So far, the idea remained a remote dream. The weather was chilly most of the year, the island was located in the path of most North Atlantic storms, and the growing season was short. Few cattle had thrived, and the only men who had become prosperous were three or four hardy pioneers who raised sheep.

The soil itself, as the militiamen who were themselves farmers quickly confirmed, was suitable only for growing a little corn and barley. So it was not surprising that a delegation of Cape Breton Island farmers called on

General Pepperrell about a month after the landing, and presented him with a petition.

"French merchant ships are no longer able to bring us the food we need in order to live," they wrote. "Through no fault of our own we are caught between opposing forces in a war that is not of our making. We have tried to remain neutral, and have offered no opposition to the subjects of King George II.

"Is the hunger of our sons and daughters the reward for our refusal to take up arms on behalf of our own King Louis?

"We beg your Honor, in humanity's name, to give us the food our families need."

Admiral du Chambon learned of the communication from one of his espionage agents, who regularly slipped back and forth through the lines west of Louisburg. It was the first encouraging news he had received in many days. Although he was being forced to feed the people of the town, the six hundred farmers, their wives and children, would cause an even greater drain on the resources of the enemy.

The petition disturbed William Pepperrell, a humane man who had a family of his own. He had no desire to cause innocent civilians to suffer unnecessary hardships, but he had too little food for his own troops. He spent an evening cursing the contractors who had swindled him; then he had himself rowed out to *Vigilant* for a conference with Commodore Warren. Sir Peter's attitude was that of a professional fighting man who could allow himself little sympathy for anyone French.

"I told Pepperrell straight out," he noted in his log, "that I have no hogsheads of grain or barrels of beef or any victuals of any sort whatever for beggars."

The best way to solve the dilemma, Warren said, would be to send the farmers and their families across the narrow Strait of Canso at the southwestern tip of Cape

Breton Island. Once they reached the mainland, which the French knew as Acadia and the British called Nova Scotia, the welfare of the unfortunates would become the concern of the government of New France.

"I could not accept the callous advice of Sir Peter," Pepperrell wrote in his journal. "Nova Scotia is a wild and barren land, inhabited in the main by bloodthirsty savages who delight in the torture and scalping of all Europeans. It is my understanding that only a few small French settlements are located there; hence, even should the refugees find their way to these towns, the people thereof have slender resources of their own, and could not give them sustenance."

The delegation of farmers remained overnight at the American camp, under guard. Pepperrell realized he had to tell them something, and early the following morning he summoned his colonels to one of the most extraordinary councils of war ever held in the New World.

The other Americans felt as he did, but could offer no practical suggestions. The corps' supplies of food were already running dangerously low, and it would be a gamble to part with enough provisons to meet the needs of almost two thousand civilians. The officers considered sending a fleet to Governor Shirley, asking for provisions, but they knew the plan was unsound. Shirley had responded at once to the request for additional gunpowder and shot, it was true, but he would need a much longer period to accumulate food stores.

What was more, the citizens of Massachusetts Bay and other colonies, who were remote from the scene of action, might well resent such a generous act of charity. The same tax system was used in each of the British colonies: ordinary expenses were paid by import and export taxes, and property assessments were made to finance the war. Since a relatively few men owned enough property to be taxed more than a token sum, the financial burden of the war was being carried by a handful of the wealthy.

Many of these men were the friends, relatives, and neighbors of the high-ranking officers, who knew there would be howls of protest at the idea of feeding the civilians of Cape Breton Island. Lieutenant Richard P. Gridley of New York told the council that his brother-in-law, a prosperous lawyer and merchant, had protested when he had been forced to pay a property tax for the support of the New York militia contingent.

"He would refuse, I know," Gridley was reported as saying, according to General Pepperrell's journal, "to give a ha'penny more for any Frenchmen, or for their children."

Others echoed his sentiments.

The impatient Colonel Vaughan listened to the talk until he could tolerate no more. Rising from the upended keg he was using as a seat, he made a few pungent remarks. In his strongbox, he said, he was carrying three hundred guineas in gold. He would contribute the entire sum, at once, to a fund for the purchase of fresh supplies. Two-thirds would be used for food needed by the troops, and the rest would be given to the Cape Breton Island civilians.

General Pepperrell, perhaps the only man present whose wealth was greater than Vaughan's, immediately said he would contribute five hundred guineas. General Waldo gave two hundred. Virtually every officer present pledged his own support.

Vaughan took charge of the project, obtaining from Commodore Warren the release of three old brigs that had been used as troop transports. These vessels, manned by colonial crews, were dispatched to Boston. An assistant supply master for the corps was on board one of the ships, and was instructed to buy as much food as he

could, as quickly as possible, and to return with it to
Cape Breton Island without delay.

The local French farmers were overwhelmed by the
unexpected personal generosity of the men who, after
all, were responsible for their plight. Two of the five
delegates promptly swore that henceforth they would be
loyal to Great Britain. They demonstrated their words
by telling General Pepperrell that espionage agents were
moving freely in and out of Louisburg, and that Admiral
du Chambon was fully informed concerning all of the
invaders' problems.

Acting on the information given him by the farmers,
Pepperrell sent several squads of scouts into the woods
west of the town of Louisburg. There three agents were
caught making their way down a ravine thickly lined with
evergreens. All three were handed over to Commodore
Warren for safekeeping, and were locked in the hold of
the *Vigilant*.

It was General Pepperrell's intention to try them before
a court-martial board, and, almost inevitably, hang them.
When the campaign ended, however, he chose instead
to exercise his prerogative as commander in chief, and
granted pardons to all three.

At the end of May, brigs returned from Boston with
enough food to alleviate the shortage being suffered by
both the corps and the island's farmers. Governor Shirley,
the assistant supply master revealed, had made a substantial contribution to the cause when he had been
informed of the mission, and so had a number of Boston's
prominent citizens. Thomas Hancock not only paid a sum
out of his own pocket for the purpose, but refused to
accept a commission on any of the provisions bought
through his office.

Men in London marveled when news of these acts of
philanthropy reached England. Never had anyone there

heard of officers not only supplying the needs of their troops out of their own purses, but buying food for enemy civilians as well.

Although neither the invaders nor the French civilians who lived beyond the Louisburg perimeter were going hungry, the corps was plagued by innumerable other problems. One of the most serious was that of finding adequate supplies of drinking water for four thousand men. Paradoxically, the marshy plain on which the militia-men were encamped was fed by a number of small streams, some of which sprang from underground sources.

However, men who drank the water from these rivulets invariably became ill. When two of them died after suffering agonizing pains for a day and a night, General Pepperrell, acting on the advice of the regimental surgeons, issued a firm order. No member of the expedition was permitted to drink water from any source in the immediate vicinity of the camp.

Other water had to be found. Scouts were sent to search for it, and finally located a large lake in the southwestern portion of the island. Unfortunately, the lake was too far from the bivouac for men to use its waters, as an all-day march was required to reach its shores.

Captain Edward Tyng of the *Massachusetts* finally worked out a satisfactory way of handling the problem. His ship, which was large enough and strong enough to beat off attacks by sloops or schooners from Quebec, sailed around the southern shore of Cape Breton Island to the lake, making the short voyage twice weekly. On board, in addition to the crew, were approximately three hundred militiamen, carrying every empty barrel and hogshead in the American camp.

These containers were filled with water and carried back to the bivouac. And once the system began to operate smoothly, there was not only enough water to drink, but the troops were able to wash their clothes as well.

A lack of adequate housing facilities was still another cause for concern. Most of the tenting the invaders carried with them was made of inferior cloth, and the workmanship had been poor. The tents leaked when rain fell, and strong winds literally ripped the shelters apart. Less than two weeks after the expedition landed, most of the tents had become useless, and the disgusted militiamen threw them away.

Thereafter the majority of the troops slept in the open, completely exposed to the elements. The nights were chilly, no matter how hot and humid the days. And the blankets in which the men wrapped themselves soaked up the moisture from the damp ground. It was small wonder that, at one time or another, virtually everyone suffered from what later generations would call severe head colds.

"Not once in all the weeks we have been here," Sergeant Ezekiel Dimmock of New London, Connecticut, wrote to his wife in late May, "have I been truly dry. The damp rot has settled into my clothing, and nothing will dry it. By day I sweat, and at night the swamp soaks me. Some of the boys have stopped washing their shirts and smallclothes, which drip like the walls of a well, ever after, after being immersed in water.

"Pity John Collins, my dear. There was no more fastidious beau in all New London before we sailed to this island. Now John looks like a ragged scarecrow. The wetness of his attire so unsettled him that he tried drying his clothes at a cooking fire, and scorched his shirt, which no longer covers his nakedness."

Attempts were made to build log cabins similar to those the frontiersmen had constructed in the English colonies, but the materials at hand were unsuitable for the purpose. There were few oaks, elms, giant beech, and maples. Most of the trees in the forest adjoining the plain were evergreens with thin, almost spindly, trunks, and so many were needed to make a single hut that the militiamen soon gave up their efforts to build themselves comfortable dwellings.

Few of the troops had traveled to New France with more than the clothing on their backs, and when shirts or breeches rotted, were badly torn, or otherwise damaged, there were no replacements for them. "We look," General Waldo wrote to his brother, "like an army of beggars."

The senior officers fared infinitely better than the captains, lieutenants, and enlisted men, however. Most had sailed north with several uniforms in their leather traveling boxes. And their tents, far more expensive than those supplied to the troops, remained whole and relatively waterproof.

Every man who spent any time ashore, with the exception of the artillerymen stationed in the Grand and Royal Batteries, was forced to undergo excruciating discomfort of another sort. The marshes of the plain were natural breeding grounds for gnats, mosquitoes, and flies that Sergeant Dimmock described as being "huge monsters, as large as moths." Since little was known about sanitation in the eighteenth century and garbage was dumped behind each battalion's sleeping area, the flies congregated there, too.

At noon, when the breeze usually died down for a few hours, the gnats appeared in such large numbers that clouds of them filled the air over the camp. Men were forced to cover their mouths and noses with handkerchiefs and strips of cloth, and on some days all activities had to be suspended until a breeze sprang up again and blew the gnats away.

A few men developed an immunity to mosquitoes, and were not troubled. But the majority remained miserable, and went about their duties with swollen faces, arms, and legs. The flies were even more vicious, leaving angry red welts on human bodies when they bit. "The Pennsylvanians have the misfortune to be living near a bog," Sergeant Dimmock wrote to his wife. "There the clusters of mosquitoes and giant flies are so thick that we believe some of their troops may soon go mad. Day and night men itch from their scalps to the soles of their feet, and no remedy the surgeons have devised offers them relief."

The farmers of Cape Breton Island who had become friendly with the Americans told them that the Louisburg garrison warded off insects by burning incense. Unfortunately, there was not a single, pungent stick in the entire camp. "There are days," General Pepperrell wrote in his journal, "when we dread the hum of insects more than the roar of French artillery. Were it not for the blessed relief offered us on occasion by the sea winds that disperse the plaguing creatures for a time, we would have no choice but to abandon our campaign and sail for home."

By far the most dangerous and debilitating of the Americans' troubles was an illness that some called "camp fever" and others referred to as "swamp fever." Physicians of later periods, trying to diagnose the disease by its symptoms, have remained puzzled. Men developed a high fever, could retain no food for days, and lay helplessly on their blankets while severe pains and cramps shot up and down their arms and legs.

It is possible that the ailment was a form of malaria, carried by the mosquitoes, but only two or three men actually died, and those who survived were immune to the disease thereafter. So, in all probability, the sickness was not malaria. Modern medicine cannot be certain whether, in fact, insects were carriers, and it is impossible to determine whether the disease was contagious.

Whatever its nature, until the very end of the campaign it made a shambles of the American corps. More than two thousand men, approximately half of the little army, were stricken. The effectiveness of the corps was reduced appreciably, and strenuous efforts were made to conceal the invaders' weakness from the enemy. Had the French known of their plight, Admiral du Chambon might have ordered his troops to attack and drive them from the island.

Among those who suffered from the fever were General Waldo and Colonel Vaughan, and Waldo sent a graphic account of the experience to his brother. "For three days and nights," he wrote, "I prayed for death so I would be released from my agony. My vision was so badly blurred that I could see nothing more than a few feet from me. One morning, when one of the physicians who attended me daily was bending over me, I did not recognize him until his face was close to mine.

"The fever consumed me, and the very thought of food made me feel worse. My limbs were on fire, and for many days after the fever subsided, they were so sore that I wanted to weep when something touched them.

"My worst anguish was suffered in the days after the fever subsided and the physicians told me I was cured. I was so weak I could scarcely stand, and when I spent as long as one hour in the saddle making an inspection of the troops, I felt so faint that I had to be carried to my bed, there to sleep for the rest of the day."

The sailors, both English and American, were spared, as were troops stationed in the captured batteries. So it is reasonable to assume that living conditions on the swampy plain were responsible for the disease. In time, the ailment was called, "Louisburg fever," and a variety of sicknesses were known by that name until the eve of the American Revolution.

General Pepperrell had to cope with still another problem, one that the Duke of Marlborough, a generation earlier, had described vividly. "The army that conducts a siege," the great English soldier had written, "is prey to boredom. There is no escape from it. Men lose their appetites for food and spirits, and cannot sleep. Good friends snarl at one another, and the soldiers of one company are sometimes known to knife those of another, in the night. They feel a malice toward all who cross their paths, the enemy remaining locked behind the walls of his city. Some generals order sorties against the defenders, hoping that a bath of blood will calm their troops, but I do not hold with this device."

Pepperrell did not approve of the technique either, although the quarrels in the American camp were becoming virulent. Old rivalries between the colonies were renewed, and there was a riot between men from Massachusetts Bay and others from Connecticut that was particularly vicious. Six soldiers were injured, and a captain from New Hampshire who tried to stop the fight was beaten unconscious. A few days later, the Pennsylvanians and Virginians began to club each other with the butts of their rifles, and firearms might have been discharged in anger if the convalescing General Waldo had not arrived on the scene during a routine inspection tour. Even he found it difficult to calm the troops.

Dissension appeared in the high command, too. General Pepperrell felt that the soldiers were carrying more than their fair share of the burden, while Commodore Warren declared that only the efforts of his seamen prevented the collapse of the entire effort. The two leaders quarreled bitterly in Sir Peter's suite on board the *Vigilant* while dining together one evening, and their aides could hear the sounds of their loud, angry voices.

Fortunately, both were sensible men, and quickly made their peace with each other. But the strain of starving a determined enemy into submission continued to weigh heavily on the entire invading force.

10

"The battle of Louisburg," wrote Colonel Hanscomb of Rhode Island, "is being fought by the artillery alone. They fire and we reply. We fire and they reply. Regiments of foot may have their place in war, but dwarves must hide in some remote, secure corner when giants clash."

The French enjoyed many advantages in the long-range duel. The great fort they were defending had been constructed for the express purpose of withstanding a siege, and the defenders had every reason to feel confident that the investment would fail. Most of the shots fired by the Rhode Island militiamen and the Royal Navy gunners did them little harm. Even the twenty-four-pounders captured by the enemy inflicted only minor damage. Stones were chipped, of course, and occasionally one cracked to a depth of eight or ten inches, but the walls remained upright and intact. Nowhere were there holes, nowhere did the bastions crumble.

Admiral du Chambon knew, as did the invaders, that a massed infantry attack on the Citadel would be suicidal. Equally important, he was convinced that the defenders were capable of holding out virtually indefinitely. Du Chambon's records indicate that there was enough food in the fort's underground storage bins to feed the garrison and the civilians of the town for many months and that the cellar munitions vaults were still piled high with powder and shot. And, more important than any other factor, the spirits of the French soldiers remained high.

Every afternoon, when the setting of the sun silenced

the guns on both sides, the French conducted an elaborate, mocking ritual. The officers and soldiers who had been manning the French guns gathered on the twin turrets overlooking the plain to the south. Since they were beyond rifle range, they came out into the open.

Serving maids appeared in starched aprons of spotless white. Some were members of the personal household staffs of Admiral du Chambon and other high-ranking officials, while a few were young women of the town recruited for the purpose of taunting the enemy. The men were handed glasses, which the girls filled with wine.

Then the artillerymen lined the parapets, facing toward the south. Raising their arms high, they drank toasts to the enemy. The Americans, seeing the gestures although unable to hear the taunting laughter that accompanied them, went off to suppers of parched corn and jerked beef, uncomfortable nights on the wet ground, and cups of stale water that had been brought to them at great inconvenience by the *Massachusetts*.

"We sometimes wonder," Captain John Grant of Fort Albany, New York, wrote to his parents, "whether we or the French are under siege. When the breeze blows from the direction of the Citadel, we smell the delicious odors of their cooking as we sit around our dismal fires. You will understand, I know, why all of us hate the north wind."

The invaders could use few of the siege tactics that had been standard procedures for thousands of years. Had General Pepperrell been able to employ these techniques, he would have moved his lines closer to the Citadel, inch by inch, day by day. In this way, eventually, he could have squeezed the life out of the garrison and forced Admiral du Chambon to surrender. But the artillery of the French, which overwhelmingly outnumbered his own gunnery strength and that of Commodore Warren, kept him at a distance.

5   Sketch of the frigate *Massachusetts* from JOURNAL OF THE LATE
SIEGE BY THE TROOPS FROM NORTH AMERICA, James Gibson,
London, 1745.

6   Portrait of Governor William Shirley of Massachusetts.   *Courtesy of
the Massachusetts Art Commission.*

7   View of Louisburg in 1731 by Verrier.   *Courtesy of the Public Archives of Canada.*

5   Sketch of the frigate *Massachusetts* from JOURNAL OF THE LATE
SIEGE BY THE TROOPS FROM NORTH AMERICA, James Gibson,
London, 1745.

6   Portrait of Governor William Shirley of Massachusetts.   *Courtesy of
the Massachusetts Art Commission.*

7   View of Louisburg in 1731 by Verrier.   *Courtesy of the Public Archives of Canada.*

8   Portrait of Sir Peter Warren, attributed to John Smibert.   *Courtesy of the Portsmouth (N. H.) Athenaeum.*

9   Portrait of Lord Jeffrey, First Lord of Amherst. *Courtesy of the Bettmann Archive.*

Realizing that the Rhode Island artillerymen were bearing a burden far greater than their experience warranted, Pepperrell arranged with Sir Peter to borrow some expert Royal Navy gunners. When the sailors came ashore to man the cannon, the marksmanship improved, with many shots clearing the walls of the Citadel.

It was decided at a council of war that the fort might be more vulnerable from the side where the town lay than anywhere else. So a number of guns were moved into the forest west of Louisburg, a task that required skill, strength, and patience. These batteries opened a steady fire on the Citadel, but the sights of the gunners were obscured by evergreens, and most of the shots fell short, landing in the town. Several civilians were killed; the exact number of casualties was never revealed.

The rest of the townspeople fled into the Citadel for protection. They and the troops of the garrison were outraged by what they believed had been a deliberate, barbaric attempt to cow the defenders.

Commodore Warren then conceived another plan. He sent his bomb ketch, a small, sturdy ship, through the inner harbor late one dark evening. Its mission was the planting of bombs that would destroy sections of the lowest part of the wall. If these twenty-foot ramparts crumbled, the militiamen could enter the Citadel with ease.

The ketch, its sails furled, was rowed to the inner end of the harbor, and every precaution was taken. The ship hugged the shore, oarlocks were muffled with cloth and absolute silence was maintained on board. When it reached its goal, almost under the noses of the sentries pacing on the wall, six men went ashore in the ketch's boat, intending to plant the bombs at the base of the wall.

But Admiral du Chambon was too experienced a sailor to be caught off guard by this ploy. He had been anticipating it for many days, and infantry marksmen, firing through slits in the wall, killed the six sailors before they could light the fuses on the bombs. At the same time the Citadel's smaller cannon opened such a furious bombardment that the ketch was almost literally blown out of the water.

She limped back to the outer lip of the harbor, enduring a cascade of steady fire all the way. When she finally reached the shelter of the frigates, it was found that there were only seven survivors out of a crew of twenty-three. And the ketch had been damaged so severely that she had to be almost completely rebuilt before she would be seaworthy again.

Meanwhile several French defenders had come out of the fort and disassembled the bombs still lying on the ground, rendering them harmless. So Commodore Warren's efforts failed as miserably as had General Pepperrell's.

The two commanders of the invasion force sat down together to review their situation, and Sir Peter noted in his log, "We grasped at straws."

Pepperrell, the more optimistic of the pair, was stubbornly cheerful. He wrote in his log, "We studied the advantages we have gained."

Both men had to search for "advantages." A few days earlier a civilian, a tailor of about forty, had escaped from the Citadel, and had been questioned at length. He had said that the residents of the town were grieving for their lost homes, and that their low spirits were infecting the garrison. The French troops, he declared, were heartily sick of the siege, and Admiral du Chambon was so well aware of their attitude that he was promising the soldiers bonuses and other rewards if they would continue to hold out.

Taken at face value, the tailor's story was encouraging. But it was impossible for either Pepperrell or Warren to determine whether he was a genuine defector or whether the French had sent him into the enemy camp.

It was difficult to imagine why Admiral du Chambon would want his enemies to think that morale was deteriorating inside the Citadel. Perhaps, Warren and Pepperrell reasoned, he assumed they knew it was difficult to keep up morale during a siege and consequently felt it wise to admit he had been having his troubles, while emphasizing the fact that they were being overcome.

Other advantages the invaders enjoyed were negligible. Warren was afraid a strong squadron of French warships might soon appear. And Pepperrell had already obtained evidence that the Micmac warriors of Abbé le Loutre might arrive momentarily. Militia scouts operating in the forests of the western portion of Cape Breton Island had surprised two warriors, who had been killed after a brief fight. Both had been identified by their war paint as Micmac.

There were other nagging worries, too. Colonel Vaughan, who had been ordered to make preparations for the day when a direct assault could be made on the Citadel, had replied with a negative report. The scaling ladders that had been made in Boston and New York Town were ten to twenty feet too short. Since they had been constructed of hardwood and iron, it was impossible for the expedition's carpenters to fashion new, longer ladders, neither the tropical wood nor the metal for the purpose being available. Vaughan had experimented by lashing two ladders together, but said they were unstable, and might fall apart if large numbers of men climbed them.

Supplies of medicines were running low, as so much had been used by the physicians during the plague of swamp fever. Laudanum, an opiate given to relieve pain, was desperately needed, and would be sorely missed if a major battle took place.

What gave Commodore Warren his greatest concern was his precarious blockade of the island. He had too few sloops and schooners to keep watch on the entire coastline. So far he had been lucky, but some day the French would smuggle large quantities of fresh supplies to the defenders. Meanwhile the invaders would again run short of both food and ammunition within the next few weeks.

Therefore, Sir Peter argued, there were two basic alternatives. He urged the militia to storm and take the Citadel at once. But, if General Pepperrell did not deem such an attempt feasible, the entire enterprise should be abandoned. Warren thought it far better to retire with honor than simply to await the inevitable catastrophe.

The commander in chief of the militia declined to put his regiments in such great jeopardy. What he would and could do, he said, would be to make a fresh survey of Louisburg's defenses.

The morning after this discussion, he and General Waldo, accompanied by a number of colonels, began a tour around the entire fort. They paused frequently to examine the massive walls, high turrets, and almost innumerable guns. Somewhere, somehow, they had to find a weakness in the seemingly invincible armor of Louisburg.

They had to keep several factors in mind. Paramount was their need for a quick, key victory. Either an extension or an intensification of the siege would avail them nothing. What they sought was a bastion they could assault with some fair hope of attaining a victory that would weaken the enemy and enable the invaders to capture the fort itself within a reasonably short period.

They could not allow themselves to forget that the Micmac and the regiment of French Regulars from Quebec might arrive at any moment. In fact, they were surprised that these vital reinforcements had not yet appeared. "Our well-being, our very survival is threatened by the ever-present storm cloud of doubt that hangs over us," General Pepperrell had written in his journal only a few days earlier. "We have been praying that we might regain

our full strength before a new foe forces us to fight on
a new field of battle. Why have these French regiments
and their allies not yet crossed the Straits? Why have
they not yet engaged us in combat? We conjecture, but
in vain. Surely they will come at any time."

Of longer-range concern was the weather. It was now
June, and General Pepperrell realized that only two months
of good weather remained. Heavy rains would begin in
August, followed by violent storms in September, and
when these storms arrived, the expedition would have to
admit defeat.

Ever conscious of the pressures facing them, constantly
aware of the imminence of total failure, the members of
the American high command studied every section of
Louisburg's walls, every turret, every artillery battery. The
architects who had planned the fort had made good their
boast: the Citadel had no real weaknesses.

One portion of the defense line in particular fascinated
the invaders. At the inner end of the harbor, not far
from the spot where the ill-fated bomb ketch had met
disaster, was the single strongest link in Louisburg's armor.
It was called the Island Battery, and it had been carved
out of sheer rock on a peninsular appendage to the mainland that jutted out just beyond the walls of the Citadel
itself.

The Island Battery stood adjacent to a section of twenty-
foot wall, and although passages connected it with the
main fort, it was a separate entity. Commodore Warren
believed that the passages leading into the Citadel proper
could be sealed off in some manner, perhaps by ex-
ploding a quantity of gunpowder.

The function of the Island Battery, which it performed
brilliantly, was that of keeping enemy ships at a distance.
Even though the entrance to the harbor was in Sir
Peter's hands, the cannon of the Island Battery prevented
him from sailing closer.

The bastion was more that one hundred and fifty yards long, with a width of seventy-five feet at one side and a little more than fifty at the other. Thirty powerful cannon, all of them twenty-four-pounders, were permanently emplaced behind natural stone façades. The English frigates and the *Vigilant* had pounded the site incessantly, but had scarcely made a dent in the rock. The cave remained intact, and the muzzles of the guns still peered out across the harbor, sentinels capable of blowing a whole fleet of enemy warships out of the water.

Beyond the wider side of the Island Battery stretched a spit of low-lying land which, conceivably, might be used as a landing place in a storming operation. But this area was covered by four twelve-pounder cannon and an undetermined number of lighter, smaller guns. So any troops that tried to come ashore onto the land there would be subjected to heavy fire.

The Island Battery was capable of sustaining itself for many weeks. It had its own arsenal and storage quarters, all of them blasted out of solid rock. The French had never made a secret of the impregnability of the bastion's powder magazine, and before the outbreak of the war it had been common knowledge that even a series of direct artillery strikes on the roof of the cave above the spot where the powder magazine was located would do no harm and would leave the gunpowder intact.

Still, the members of the American high command found themselves pondering the idea of attacking the Island Battery. At first glance, the notion seemed insane, but Colonel William Vaughan, who had conceived the plan, pointed out that the capture of such a strong point in Louisburg's defenses would more than accomplish the immediate objectives of the corps. If the Battery's guns were silenced, the British and American colonial warships could sail much closer to the walls of the Citadel, and, by lobbing their shots over them, could create havoc in the

camp of the defenders. Equally important, the loss of the
key stronghold, which King Louis himself had often called
invincible, would be a crushing blow to French morale.

There were logical factors in favor of the enterprise. The
scaling ladders the Americans had carried with them were
long enough for troops to climb them and scramble through
the gunports into the interior of the Battery. And no one
could argue with Colonel Vaughan's assertion that the
Island Battery was the last place the defenders would
expect an assault.

General Pepperrell took the suggestion under advise-
ment, and conferred privately with Commodore Warren
and General Waldo. "The scheme," Sir Peter wrote in
his log, "is so mad it might succeed, provided enough
men of great courage carry it out, under the direction
of the most competent of officers."

Pepperrell decided to take the risk, and asked for volunteers. More than four hundred militiamen responded.
Troops from every colony taking part in the campaign
were included in the group, so the attack would be a
truly intercolonial enterprise. The members of the high
command were pleased.

Colonel Vaughan, who had already enjoyed such great
success in a storming operation, was named the commander
of the assault. It was fitting that he should be given
the post, since he had initiated the idea.

Then, unexpectedly, old rivalries between the colonies
flared. The troops refused to accept Vaughan as their
leader. The Maine District, they said, had won more than
its fair share of glory during the invasion, and now it was
the turn of others.

Ever since the formation of the first American militia
units in Virginia, in 1608, it had been the privilege of
colonial troops to elect their own leaders. General Pepperrell pleaded with the men to relent, but not even he had

the authority to force them to accept a commander they didn't want.

The chagrined and embarrassed William Vaughan was compelled to withdraw, which placed the entire plan in jeopardy. However, the volunteers showed their common sense in electing Colonel Brian Gorham of Connecticut as their leader. He seemed eminently suitable for the position. A frontier dweller who lived on the Connecticut River near the Massachusetts Bay border, he was already commanding an intercolonial unit, the scouts, or rangers, whose ranks were filled by other wilderness men.

Pepperrell and Waldo thought the choice a good one. Vaughan, according to the commander in chief's journal, graciously congratulated his successor and wished him every success.

The volunteers mustered at the Grand Battery, and were supplied with a small fleet of longboats. Oars would make too much noise cutting through the water, so Colonel Gorham insisted that the troops manning the boats use Indian paddles instead. Then, very quietly, he weeded out the obvious incompetents and replaced them with scouts from his own regiment. In all, one hundred and fifty of his hard-bitten rangers would form the core of the assault force.

Obviously a dark night would be needed for the operation, but the weather seemed to conspire against the invaders. With everything in readiness for the attack, the sky remained cloudless night after night, and tensions became almost unbearable. The members of the assault force spent their days and nights waiting at the Grand Battery, with nothing to occupy them.

Then late one afternoon in the first days of June, shortly before sundown, a light rain began to fall, and conditions nightfall, and General Pepperrell, arriving at the Grand Battery with General Waldo, gave the order to begin the appeared more favorable. The rain persisted long after operation a little before midnight. There was a quiet, last-minute flurry as weapons were checked and the scaling ladders were placed in the bottoms of the longboats.

Gorham's scouts, as always, were superbly well-disciplined, but the conduct of some of the other volunteers was questionable. General Waldo remarked to the commander in chief, as Pepperrell noted in his journal, "I doubt whether straggling fellows, three, four, or seven out of a company, ought to go on such service."

Neither of the generals intervened, however, believing that the reckless bravado of the militiamen had been caused by their tensions, and would pass once the operation actually began. It had not occurred to either, or to Colonel Gorham, that these troops had smuggled a keg of rum into their quarters in the Grand Battery, and had been drinking heavily to steady their nerves.

This foolish and short-sighted disobedience of basic military orders remained undetected, and at midnight the operation began, precisely on schedule. "The night had grown very dark," Colonel Gorham later wrote. "The wind had become quite intense, which caused me some concern, but the longboats were paddled silently to the innermost point of the harbor without the knowledge of the enemy. I had every reason to feel optimistic, and believed our plan well might succeed."

One hundred and fifty members of the vanguard, most of them Gorham's own scouts, were the first to climb ashore on the narrow spit of land that was the one place in the vicinity of the Island Battery on which no fortifications had been built. These men held the beach until the rest of the party landed, and then advanced cautiously toward the forbidding walls, which loomed ahead in the dark.

The French sentries apparently were asleep and raised no alarm. Colonel Gorham, increasingly encouraged, ordered his howitzers brought ashore. At the appropriate moment these guns would fire "grape," that is, small chunks of metal which would rise high in the air and then rain down on the defenders, driving them from their positions at the top of the wall.

The members of the advance guard reached the walls. Working with silent intensity, they put their scaling ladders together, lashing the sections with strips of rawhide rope. As nearly as the officers could judge, these ladders reached the top of the wall. What surprised Colonel Gorham was that the cannon capable of ripping his landing party to shreds appeared to be unmanned. If the French gun crews were anywhere near their weapons, they, too, were obviously asleep.

Americans with rifles slung across their backs, pistols in their belts, and knives in their boot tops began the long, silent climb up the ladders. Some of their comrades remained below, straining to steady the swaying, insecure ladders. The assault troops moved in unison, slowly, so they would reach the top simultaneously.

Gorham and the members of his staff peered up through the gloom, watching the military miracle that was taking place. A second wave of troops moved into position to follow the first, and there was now every reason to believe that the Island Battery would be taken by storm.

Then a loud, thick voice broke the silence. "Down with the French! Three cheers for our lads!" One of the militiamen who had consumed too much rum was shouting at the top of his voice.

"I felt," Colonel Gorham later wrote, "as though I had been immersed in the icy waters of the harbor. But I was helpless, as were my subordinates. Before anyone could reach the man who was giving away our presence to the foe, he cheered lustily, thrice."

The French had no idea what was happening, but the attackers had lost the precious advantage of surprise. Somewhere on the musket platform behind the top of the ramparts, a sentry fired his weapon. All at once the entire Island Battery came to life.

The shots of other sentries followed the first, and men could be heard running and shouting behind the walls. A moment later wads of flaming paper that had been soaked in oil and set on fire were thrown over the walls. By their light the defenders were able to see the men on the ladders, the others waiting below, the militiamen still moving ashore from the boats.

The Louisburg professionals realized they faced a severe crisis, and met it with swift, efficient action. Barrels of oil kept on the musket platform for use in just such an emergency were set on fire and poured down onto the men scaling the ladders. Cannoneers who had been asleep beside their loaded guns opened an intense barrage, raking the men at the base of the ladders, those crossing the beach, and those still in the boats.

Lieutenant Harvey Wilcox, a scout officer from New London, Connecticut, described the scene in a letter he subsequently wrote to his parents. "We had been plunged with sudden and unexpected horror into the depths of Hell itself. Some of our boys on the ladders had become flaming torches, and fell to their deaths below, screaming in agony. Our marksmen bravely opened fire on the defenders, but their shots failed to penetrate the stout walls, and did no harm other than to chip away small bits of stone. Meanwhile the guns already trained on the little beach pounded us without mercy. I find it impossible to estimate how much iron was hurled at us within a short period."

The French, too, used "grape," and small pieces of metal caused so many injuries that the effectiveness of the attacking force was substantially reduced within a few moments. Calm and relentless, the French troops maintained an unceasing barrage.

Colonel Gorham made a brief attempt to sustain the

initiative he had gained. But it quickly became obvious that he could achieve nothing. The enemy enjoyed complete protection behind the walls of the Island Battery, while his own troops were exposed. Again and again militiamen tried to scale the ladders, but were either burned by the flaming oil or driven back to the ground by musket fire from the ramparts. Some of the French gunners were concentrating their fire on the American howitzers, which had not yet been moved into position, and the accuracy of the cannoneers was remarkable. At least seven of the fourteen howitzers were rendered useless.

The stubborn bravery of the Americans was astonishing. Men who had never before fought in battle refused to panic. Troops kept their company lines, in spite of the heavy, mounting casualties. And even the wounded who were able to function returned the enemy fire.

Realizing that his entire party would be killed unless he retreated, Gorham gave the command to withdraw. The retreat, too, was orderly, although it was accomplished under the most difficult of conditions. Some of the wounded had been so badly hurt that they had to be carried to the boats. And when the French saw that the attackers were leaving, the Island Battery's cannon were turned on the frail craft, sinking a number of them and drowning the occupants.

The first streaks of dawn were appearing in the sky when Brian Gorham, the last to leave the beach, wearily climbed into a boat. He made a perfect target, and the French, still using oil-soaked wads of paper as flares, recognized him as an officer of high rank. But the commandant of the Island Battery, in a grim gesture to his opponent, ordered his own men to cease fire. Colonel Gorham was allowed to escape unharmed.

It was impossible to estimate the scope of the disaster until the dazed survivors paddled back to the harbor entrance, where the anxious Pepperrell and Waldo were waiting. They, like all other members of the expedition, were shocked by the casualty count. In all, one hundred and ninety-three men had been killed or drowned. Perhaps some of the most severely wounded had been inadvertently left behind, in which case they had presumably been made prisoners by the French.

This guess was subsequently confirmed. Fourteen badly injured Americans had been taken into the Island Battery before being transferred to the Citadel. They were given the best available medical treatment, an honor rarely accorded enemies in eighteenth-century warfare. Admiral du Chambon, in a report to King Louis, explained his generosity by saying, "The English Provincials were worthy foes, and I felt it only right to salute them."

In spite of the care given the prisoners, six of the fourteen died. The remaining eight were transferred to a dungeon when they were sufficiently recovered, and remained there until the end of the campaign.

Meanwhile, the casualties in the American bivouac continued to mount. Some of the injured died. Some required surgery, and those who had an arm or a leg amputated were no longer fit for combat and had to be sent home. Strangely, no records tallying the lists of those who died after returning to the American camp or of those who had to be sent back to the colonies have been found by historians. General Pepperrell undoubtedly made such lists and sent them to Governor Shirley, but no figures appear in the files of either man. Perhaps so many died or were permanently disabled that the actual numbers had to be kept secret in order to maintain what was left of the expedition's morale and prevent an indignant outburst at home.

One poignant note in Colonel Gorham's official report to General Pepperrell says much. "The militiaman who disclosed our presence to the French by shouting," he wrote, "was one of the first killed. Several of his comrades, believing him still alive, made valiant efforts to assist him, in hopes they could carry him to the boats. They also were killed by French marksmen."

The tragic defeat cast a heavy pall over the American camp. For the first time men began to complain that they had been sent to Cape Breton Island on a fool's errand. These malcontents declared that Louisburg could not be captured, and wanted to return to the colonies and retire from the militia before they were killed, wounded, or taken seriously ill. Whole companies and even battalions began to petition their officers, demanding the right to leave the militia.

Pepperrell had good cause to be afraid that his troops might mutiny. "I cannot ascertain," he wrote to Governor Shirley, "how many of our men still remain loyal to our cause. But I can assure Your Excellency of this much: Few would weep were we to abandon our campaign. I, however, have no intention of turning my back upon this grand enterprise. The fortunes of war have not favored us of late, and a plan in which we put much faith was shattered. Yet I continue to cling to the hope that we shall prevail. The loss of a single battle does not signify the loss of a campaign."

The failure of the Americans to capture the Island Battery gave the French a welcome boost in spirits. Admiral du Chambon made an address to his troops, promising them victory if they would continue to show fortitude and patience. He also made a personal visit to the townspeople who were now living in the Citadel, and promised them that the enemy would soon grow too weak to keep up the fight.

One of his aides, Lieutenant Maurice de Fratel, recorded his words, and later sent them to Paris. "The British are an inferior breed, as Frenchmen have known for generations. The British colonials, although superior to their masters in numerous ways because of the strengthening influences of the New World on individuals, nevertheless are endowed with many English characteristics. One day in the very near future, I predict, the soldiers who have invaded our shores will sail away on their ships, and will never return. The might of Louisburg is too great for them, and they know that if they remain here through the months ahead, they assuredly shall perish."

To an extent, the French commander was whistling in the dark, trying to capitalize on the victory as a means of bolstering both soldiers and civilians whose basic situation was still unpleasant. Neither the reinforcements from Quebec nor the Micmac had arrived to relieve the garrison, and some of the defenders believed they had been abandoned by the authorities in the capital of New France. As a matter of fact, Admiral du Chambon was secretly troubled because no fleet had appeared to drive off Sir Peter Warren's squadron. Well aware of the rivalries at the Versailles court of King Louis, and of the short-sightedness of the Naval Board in Paris, he had good cause to fear that his colleagues wanted to take the easy route to glory by winning victories close to home.

What he did not know, and what would have heartened him immeasurably, was that there was now a real rift in the high command of the forces investing Louisburg.

11

Commodore Warren was thoroughly disgusted by the failure of the American attempt to capture the Island Battery. As a lifelong professional fighting man, he automatically held a commander responsible for the acts of his subordinates, and therefore blamed General Pepperrell for the disastrous blunder that had snatched from the militia what might have been a great victory.

The strain of the long campaign had taken its toll on Sir Peter, and Pepperrell, in spite of his determination, was also suffering from fatigue and tension. Until now, the aristocratic Englishman and the colonial merchant-farmer-soldier had worked together in a remarkably harmonious relationship, but that accord was shattered when the naval chief paid a visit to the headquarters of his military counterpart shortly after the ill-fated attack.

Virtually nothing is known of their argument. No mention of the dispute appears in Warren's log or Pepperrell's journal, but a number of officers commented in their correspondence that the sounds of a violent quarrel could be heard emanating from the General's tent. The embarrassed aides of both commanders kept everyone but General Waldo at a distance. Waldo joined his two superiors, but remained closemouthed on the subject after he emerged from the tent.

The results of the disagreement soon became apparent. Instead of holding a joint daily meeting, attended by their staffs, the two commanders avoided one another. Warren sent a strongly worded letter to Governor Shirley, saying that the campaign itself was in jeopardy. In order to attain its objectives, he wrote, the entire force should be placed under the overall command of one man. He was careful to indicate that he did not care whether he received the appointment, but he hinted, none too subtly, that he would return to England rather than place himself under the orders of a man he believed to be an amateur.

The letter confused and alarmed William Shirley. He was far from the scene, and was in no position to judge the merits of either Warren's position or Pepperrell's. His political genius was such, however, that he neatly sidestepped the issue. Whether he had the authority to appoint one man the supreme commander of the expedition was questionable. Certainly he had no right to assume the prerogatives of the crown in dealing with a high-ranking officer of the Royal Navy.

But such matters were irrelevant to the main issue, the restoration of harmony between the military and naval chiefs on Cape Breton Island. So he wrote Warren a soothing but deliberately vague letter, in which he ignored the Commodore's command. The passage of time and the pressures of events, he hoped, would heal the breach.

Sir Peter Warren was not one to brood or sulk. Impatient to bring the campaign to a successful close, he proposed a venture of his own. Although originally he had not favored an attack on the Island Battery, he convinced himself that the Citadel could be taken only if this strong outpost were first captured. Therefore, he sent Pepperrell a brief note, saying that he intended to sail across the harbor with all of his fighting ships, and that he would reduce the Battery in an artillery duel.

Pepperrell, who at the moment had only two thousand healthy men capable of bearing arms, replied calmly. He had learned of Sir Peter's letter to Governor Shirley, and offered the Commodore precisely what he wanted. Warren could take all of his troops for the attack, he said, using them in any way he saw fit.

The colonial leader's magnanimity was totally unexpected, and Warren hesitated. He would be taking grave risks if he conducted a direct assault on the Island Battery, whose guns might smash some of his ships. And, if he failed, he alone would be responsible. It was probable that, under such circumstances, the Admiralty in London would court-martial him for his recklessness. After considering the matter for a few days, Sir Peter abandoned his plan. He wrote again to Pepperrell, in a far friendlier tone, saying that even if he managed to silence the cannon of the Island Battery, he would be well within the range of the guns mounted in the Citadel itself.

"Like you," he wrote, "I prefer caution to foolhardiness."

The renewal of good relations between Pepperrell and Warren had begun before Governor Shirley in Boston received Sir Peter's angry communication demanding the supreme command.

A few days after the argument in Pepperrell's tent, a party of thirty-seven American scouts, keeping watch for the Micmac in the wilderness on the far side of Cape Breton Island, was attacked by a far larger group of Indians, commanded by French officers. Twenty of the Americans managed to escape, ten others were killed, and the remaining seven surrendered when the French officers promised them humane treatment.

As soon as they laid down their arms, however, they were seized by the Micmac warriors and put to death by slow torture. Several of their escaped comrades, although unable to intervene, witnessed the gruesome scene from their hiding places in the forest.

When these men returned to the American camp with the news, Pepperrell and Warren both felt a sense of outrage at the French that dwarfed their own differences. At

Sir Peter's request, the captured commander of the *Vigilant*, Captain Maisonfort, wrote a letter of protest to Admiral du Chambon. "It is well that you should be informed," he said, "that the Captains and officers of this squadron treat us, not as their prisoners, but as their good friends, and take particular pains that my officers and crew should want for nothing. Therefore it seems just to me to treat them in like manner, and to punish those who do otherwise and offer any insult to the prisoners that may fall into your hands."

The officer chosen by Sir Peter to deliver the communication under a flag of truce was a young lieutenant who had spent a number of years in France prior to the war, and who spoke the language fluently. However, he concealed his knowledge of French when he was admitted to the office of Admiral du Chambon. In this way he discovered that the Governor and his staff, who spoke French freely to one another in his presence, were dismayed. They had not known that the captured vessel was the *Vigilant*. In fact, they had been entertaining high hopes that she would lead a squadron to their rescue, dispersing the British.

So the lieutenant returned to Commodore Warren with news to the effect that the isolated French garrison had suffered a severe blow to their morale. He also carried several letters of reply, one to Captain Maisonfort, one to Warren, and one to Pepperrell. In each Admiral du Chambon said substantially the same thing: the Indians, not their French officers, had been responsible for the torture and massacre of the captured scouts. To the extent that he could, he would control such excesses in the future. And he took pains to point out that the American prisoners captured at the Island Battery were being well treated.

Warren and Pepperrell suspected that the presence of a large party of Indian scouts near the Strait of Canso meant that the main body of Micmac would soon be arriving on Cape Breton Island. They found a hint of confirmation, too, in Admiral du Chambon's vaguely worded promise to curb excesses when he could. Apparently he expected Indians to engage in large-scale fighting in the near future.

Pepperrell and Warren held a council of war on the *Vigilant,* and while they were trying to analyze the tidbits of information they had gleaned, a Connecticut sloop that had been on patrol duty arrived under full sail. The word she brought indicated that a major crisis was in the offing. While cruising off the lowlands of the Nova Scotia mainland, where foliage was sparse, her lookout had seen a very large body of men marching in the direction of Cape Breton Island. Her captain had climbed into the crow's-nest himself, sailing as close to the shore as he dared in order to observe the enemy formation. After keeping the enemy under close surveillance for more than a half hour, he had been driven off by cannon fire.

The captain said he estimated there were approximately eight hundred Micmac in the party. And the ranks of the warriors were vastly exceeded by those of white-clad French troops.

General Pepperrell and Commodore Warren questioned the sloop commander at length, and then made their own estimate. If his report was accurate, a force far larger than a regiment was marching to the relief of Louisburg. A conservative guess would indicate there were at least fifteen hundred French soldiers in the column.

As it happened, this estimate was not far wrong. A total of thirteen hundred of the best professional soldiers in New France were at last drawing near Cape Breton Island, under the command of Colonel Michel du Bourzt Marin, Marquis de St. Columbe, one of the ablest and most distinguished officers in the entire French army. He had left Quebec with a force of five hundred men, and had added to his brigade on the march. In fact, he had gone from one small outpost garrison to another, taking with him most of the soldiers stationed at each of them. This roundabout march accounted for the long delay in reaching his destination.

General Pepperrell and Commodore Warren had learned enough to realize that they had to act together, at once, in order to meet the gravest threat they had yet faced. If the relief force managed to reach Cape Breton Island and marched through the wilderness to the swampy plains south of Louisburg, they could attack the Americans on one front while Admiral du Chambon's troops poured out of the Citadel to assault the invaders from another side.

The naval advantage enjoyed by the British and American colonials would be of little help in a battle on the plains. The warships could not sail close to the shore because of the rocks off the coastline, and would be unable to fire on the enemy without hitting their own troops, too.

Therefore, in order to make use of the squadron, it was imperative to cut off the French and Micmac before they crossed the Strait of Canso. All of the members of the British and American high commands were aware that Marin and his troops, together with the Micmac, possessed a strength greater than Pepperrell could put into the field, so the need for immediate action was doubled.

Several problems had to be solved very quickly. Every available ship and every available soldier was needed for the attempt to intercept Colonel Marin's troops and Abbé le Loutre's Indians. But, at the same time, it was also necessary to maintain the siege of Louisburg. If too many militiamen sailed away, the French in the Citadel could storm the invaders' strong points. Similarly, if the squadron was weakened too much, Admiral du Chambon might be able to regain possession of the Royal Battery and the Grand Battery at the entrance to the harbor.

Warren and Pepperrell agreed that they had to gamble. Sir Peter decided to remain at Louisburg on the *Vigilant,* keeping the *Launceton,* the *Connecticut,* and the American sloops with him. The *Superbe,* the *Mermaid,* the *Eltham,* and the *Massachusetts* were ordered to sail off to the Strait of Canso as soon as the militia troops could be taken on board.

Pepperrell, in order to disguise the weakening of his investing force, opened a furious bombardment of the Citadel. While the cannon roared, more than twelve hundred of his two thousand able-bodied troops were carried out to the warships in boats. The force remaining at Louisburg was just strong enough to contain the French garrison for a limited time. If anything untoward happened to the ships and regiments being sent to ward off Colonel Marin and the Micmac, the entire expedition would be doomed.

In command of the naval squadron being sent to intercept the enemy was Captain Robert Robertson, commander of the *Eltham* and the senior Royal Navy officer present. General Pepperrell having elected to stay on at Louisburg with Commodore Warren, General Waldo was in command of the land forces, with Colonel Vaughan and Colonel Gorham as his deputies.

The squadron moved off toward the southwest under full sail, the *Eltham* and the *Massachusetts* in the van behind the screen of Royal Navy sloops. Waldo, Vaughan, and Gorham, traveling on Robertson's flagship, held an urgent council of war. So much had happened so quickly that it had not been possible to make any specific plans. Even now, sitting quietly in the solitude of a cabin on the rolling frigate, it was difficult to look ahead. The three officers agreed they would have to keep the situation under constant study as it developed.

In the meantime, Waldo wanted the troops kept out of the way of the busy sailors. A message to that effect was sent to the other ships. As it happened, the sea was unusually heavy, and most of the militiamen were seasick, unable to interfere with operations even had they wanted to be more active.

Captain Robertson had no battle plan, either, as he continued to drive toward the southwest through the long hours of the day and night. His squadron arrived off the Strait of Canso shortly after dawn, and he asked General Waldo to join him on his quarterdeck. There they discussed the possibility of anchoring in the Strait while some of Colonel Gorham's scouts explored the land on both sides to discover whether the enemy had yet crossed from the mainland to Cape Breton Island.

While they talked, there was a bustle of activity on the *Massachusetts*. The converted merchantman had a taller mainmast than any of the other ships, and the energetic Captain Edward Tyng could be seen kicking off his boots and climbing up to his crow's-nest. Shortly after he reached it, he shouted down to his quarterdeck, and a few moments later the *Massachusetts* broke out her signal flags. Tyng had sighted the foe gathering on the Nova Scotia side of the Strait, preparatory to crossing over to Cape Breton Island.

Robertson immediately ordered his squadron into battle formation, with the frigates in the lead and the smaller sloops bringing up the rear. Gunports were lowered, the ships were stripped for action, and the militiamen on the decks were ordered below.

"Our arrival at the Strait," General Waldo said in his official report to General Pepperrell, "was providential, and proves that the Almighty is watching over us. Had we reached the channel three or four hours later, the enemy would have crossed into the wilderness of Cape Breton Island, from whence we could not have dislodged him."

The English and American officers saw scores of small craft being carried down to the water on the mainland side of the narrow Strait. Virtually all were Indian boats that, presumably, the Micmac had made especially for this crossing. Some were canoes, slender and graceful, made of bark, and others were the snub-nosed *bateaux,* light in weight but somewhat sturdier, that were commonly used by French trappers on the St. Lawrence and other rivers of New France.

Vegetation was sparse along the shore. Grasslike reeds came down to the water's edge, and a few bushes dotted the landscape. But the stunted pines typical of this section of rocky Nova Scotia soil were a considerable distance from the shoreline, perhaps two hundred to three hundred yards. Colonel Marin's French troops and the Micmac, expecting no sudden confrontation with hostile forces, had camped in the open, the soldiers having erected neat rows of tents for themselves. The Indians, scorning cover, had slept on the ground.

A large number of breakfast campfires were still smoldering, and the white-clad French troops jumped to their feet and raced for their muskets when they caught sight of the squadron. Abbé le Loutre's warriors, needing no orders, promptly fanned out in the tall grass.

General Waldo and his deputies, studying the enemy from the quarterdeck of the *Eltham,* first thought that Colonel Marin's force was considerably larger than they had been led to expect. The tents were spread out over a considerable area, since the French hated being crowded together, and at first glance the militia chiefs believed they had stumbled onto a corps of at least three thousand men, not counting the Indian braves. Not until the battle that developed had been in progress for some time did they revise their estimates downward.

The tactics devised on the spot by Captain Robertson were simple. As each of his warships reached a position abreast of the enemy, several broadsides were fired. Birds nesting in the trees on Cape Breton Island promptly took alarmed flight, and the gulls that had been following the squadron also vanished.

But the damage done by the frigates was negligible. Ironically, their guns were too powerful to be effective at such close range. Most of the crews overshot their mark, sending their iron crashing into the distant scrub pines. Meanwhile the French scattered over a still broader area, making themselves more difficult targets to hit. The British sloops, following the larger vessels in single file, achieved somewhat greater success, since they were able to move considerably closer to the mainland shore. Also, their cannon were smaller, which made it easier for their crews to find the right range. Unfortunately, they mounted too few guns to do much damage.

Robertson ordered the squadron to tack and sail back in the opposite direction. The maneuver was difficult to achieve, partly because the Strait was so narrow, and partly because the current was strong. But all of the ships carried out the order, and the *Eltham*, repeating her original tactics, began to fire broadsides with her starboard guns.

Captain Edward Tyng was dissatisfied with the results he had achieved. Impatiently, almost recklessly, he sailed closer to the mainland shore, deliberately risking the possibility that he might damage the *Massachusetts* on the jagged, heavy rocks that dotted the side of the channel. He ordered his gun crews to lower the trajectory on their cannon to a minimum, and they fired point blank at the enemy.

The results were as devastating as the maneuver itself was startling. For the first time the French were severely mauled. And the Micmac, who had been burrowing into the soft ground, half-hidden by the reeds, promptly ran toward the relative shelter of the pines. As nearly as the officers watching from the quarterdecks of the ships could judge, the French suffered casualties of twenty to thirty men either killed or badly wounded.

The other frigates, however, were unable or unwilling

to follow Tyng's example, and Colonel Marin's troops began to move forward again after the *Massachusetts* had
passed. The basic problem of how to deal with the situation remained unsolved.

After reaching the open sea, the squadron tacked once
more, and as the ships headed back toward the Strait
under reduced sail, Captain Robertson and General Waldo
held a second brief council of war. Both were imaginative
men driven by military necessity to adopt extreme measures, and they quickly worked out a plan of action that
Commodore Warren, in his subsequent report to the Admiralty in London, called, "superb madness."

The frigates anchored in the channel, which was difficult
for them to do because of the strong tide. Then, while
they maintained a steady bombardment with their port
guns, the boats were lowered and the American militia
went ashore. The cannon fire was intended to hold the
enemy at a distance, but the French came forward far
enough to greet the militiamen with a barrage of musket
fire. Then the Micmac, taking heart, actually ran down
to the shore itself where they opened up with muskets and
rifles.

The counterattack was so strong that Waldo, who was
in one of the first boats inching toward the mainland, was
uncertain whether it might be wiser to withdraw. The
cannon fire was none too effective, and the French and
their Indian allies were giving as good as they received.

Once more Captain Tyng took matters into his own
hands. In a breathtaking exhibition of seamanship he
edged the *Massachusetts* close to the rocks. He came so
close, in fact, that a sailor from Cape Cod who was
stationed in the bow later wrote to his parents that "I
could have reached out with my hand and touched the
side of a huge sea boulder."

The port guns of the American frigate roared again,
each crew reloading as fast as possible and firing at will.

Under the murderous fire of the *Massachusetts*, the French and the Micmac were compelled to retreat from the shore.

The militia landed unopposed, and while the *Massachusetts'* cannon continued to give the troops protective cover, preventing the enemy from returning, General Waldo's men went to work. First they destroyed every canoe and *bateau* they could find, ripping the craft with bayonets, chopping them with axes, and, when no better tools were at hand, using the butts of their rifles and the soles of their heavy boots to crush the fragile bark shells.

But Waldo knew, as did Vaughan and Gorham, that a fleet of small boats could be rebuilt in a few days. What was essential in order to prevent Colonel Marin and Abbé le Loutre from reaching Louisburg was a concerted assault so deadly that it would permanently disperse the enemy.

The guns on the frigates, with the exception of those on the *Massachusetts*, raised their trajectory and began to fire a little farther inland. Meanwhile Tyng continued to hold the French and Micmac at a distance with his heavy, direct fire. The militia battalions now moved into formation and Gorham was given command of the vanguard. He sought the honor in order to erase the shame he had suffered in the futile assault on the Island Battery, and his frontiersmen were more familiar with Indian fighting techniques than were the troops of other units.

General Waldo and Captain Tyng achieved a degree of coordination that was astonishing in view of the fact that neither had ever practiced the intricate maneuver that followed. The militiamen spread out in approved wilderness fashion, leaving a space of anywhere from five to ten feet between each man. Then, as the long lines slowly advanced toward the enemy, Tyng gradually raised the level of his fire. Iron shot screamed over the heads of the militiamen as they moved forward, but the heavy gunfire prevented the French from rushing toward them and driving them into the water.

The Micmac quickly indicated they wanted no part of the battle that was developing. Totally unaccustomed to disciplined action, the savages preferred to make surprise attacks, or, when working with allies, to swarm over a confused enemy. They dispersed, some moving deep into the stands of pine, others going off a safe distance from the flanks. By no means had they permanently retired from the field, but they clearly intended to wait until the French achieved a distinct advantage before returning to the battle.

The forces of Waldo and Marin were fairly evenly matched. The French had more men in the field, but the Americans enjoyed the support of the warships' guns, so a rough balance was achieved. Certainly both commanders knew that, once they were locked in close combat, the artillery would be compelled to fall silent for fear of hitting friendly troops.

Thus Marin, with the larger and better-trained corps, augmented by the Micmac, enjoyed an ultimate advantage over his opponent. Under ordinary circumstances he should have been able to win a decisive victory. But at this critical point, when the fight was just beginning to develop, he made a serious mistake. He had two basic choices: either he spread out his troops, as the Americans were doing, or he could send his men into battle European fashion, in closely knit ranks. He elected the latter course.

His error was caused by ignorance of the true identity of his opponents, not by a lack of experience. Since most of the warships that had been bombarding his forces were Royal Navy vessels, he assumed that the troops coming ashore were also British. The news that American colonials made up the land force of the expedition attacking Louisburg had not reached Quebec at the time he had begun his march from the city, and at no time since then had he been informed that the soldiers he would meet were mere militiamen.

He was condemned by some of his critics in Paris in the years following the battle on the grounds that he should have known the truth at once. British troops, these gentlemen said, always wore scarlet uniforms, just as the French always wore white. However the charge was neither fair nor accurate. Members of the British Royal Marine Corps, the Navy's own soldiers, traditionally dressed in dark green uniforms.

The militiamen wore attire of various kinds, some of which was indeed dark green. Also, it was difficult for Colonel Marin to see his enemies clearly, since the smoke emitted by the belching cannon was rolling directly toward him, obscuring his own vision and that of his immediate subordinates. Marin therefore took it for granted that the advancing enemy soldiers were Royal Marines, professionals like his own troops.

His mistake soon proved costly. The French troops, bunched together in neat, hollow squares, made perfect targets for the American sharpshooters. The Americans, however, were difficult to hit. Their loose formation was an excellent protection, and when the French returned their fire, they unhesitatingly dropped into the reeds in order to attain better concealment.

As soon as the two land forces made direct contact, the *Massachusetts* altered her fire, and began to lob her iron over the heads of the combatants. The other frigates were already doing the same thing, which made it difficult for the French to retreat. If they moved toward the rear, they would be heading directly into the artillery fire.

But Marin's hard-bitten troops had no intention of falling back. They came forward in splendid formation, each square as precisely drawn as it would have been on a drillfield or on parade, bayonets gleaming in the summer sunlight.

The French never quite knew what hit them. Riflemen from the wilderness of Massachusetts Bay and Connecticut, Pennsylvania and Virginia, broke up the formations with what appeared to be consummate ease. The enemy soldiers doggedly reformed their ranks, closing the gaps when men fell, and continued to advance.

"Their courage was a fine tribute to their training and national characteristics," General Waldo wrote in his report to General Pepperrell. "But our boys gave them no chance and no quarter. The slaughter was sickening."

The Americans, still in their loose wilderness formation, also continued to move forward, and after less than a quarter of an hour only fifty feet separated the front lines. But the French were suffering from a grave handicap. Their lines were so tight that it was almost impossible for even the most inexperienced of the Americans to miss their shots. And the frontier sharpshooters were able to select their individual targets at will.

Colonels Vaughan and Gorham ordered their expert marksmen to concentrate on the enemy's officers and sergeants. Captains and lieutenants began to fall, but the French did not falter. Rarely, if ever, had any body of men displayed such courage in New World combat.

Finally, deprived of company leadership, the French troops became uneasy. One unit came to a halt, then another. Senior officers, who were mounted, rode forward through the lines, urging the men not to stop, but a sense of panic began to spread through the ranks when lieutenant colonels and majors toppled from their mounts to the ground.

The American fire was steady, relentless. Waldo, paying special tribute to Gorham's regiment in his report, said, "They behaved like real veterans."

Suddenly the battle was ended. The French could tolerate no more, and refusing to heed the shouted commands of their top-ranking officers, started off toward the rear.

For a few moments the withdrawal was orderly, units holding their formations. But the panic was a contagion that spread rapidly, and within a short time every man was fleeing, racing toward the shelter of the pines. Comrades were forgotten, military discipline abandoned, and what had been a proud corps became a frightened mob.

The Americans pursued them to the edge of the pine forest, but General Waldo called a halt when he realized that shot from the frigates was falling directly ahead. The French, still fleeing, were forced to take the risk of being hit by iron shot as they ran.

The Micmac were no longer a potential factor in the struggle. Abbé le Loutre made a desperate attempt to keep his braves in the field, but the senior warriors vanished as soon as it became evident that Colonel Marin would suffer a defeat, and their followers rapidly disappeared, too.

The frigates' guns were still booming, sending their shot deep inland, when General Waldo gave his regiments the order to return to the ships. The entire battle, from the time the warships had first encountered the French, had lasted no more than three hours. And the militiamen had spent little more than an hour ashore.

The results of the engagement were of the utmost significance. Colonel Marin's corps had been shattered, and his ability to take an active part in future operations on Cape Breton Island had been destroyed. He had suffered so many casualties that, General Waldo felt certain, he would be forced to return to Quebec with his wounded.

The ranks of the Micmac were intact, but the danger they posed was greatly reduced. Savages, no matter what their tribe, were generally interested only in spoils, and were unwilling to wage war unless they could be sure they were taking part on the winning side. Waldo was positive the Micmac would return to their own villages, and both Gorham and Vaughan concurred in his opinion.

The combined sea and land operation of the British and

Americans had been an overwhelming success, and the tired members of the expedition set sail for Louisburg in a jubilant mood.

Captain Robertson and General Waldo agreed that the man who deserved more credit for the victory than anyone else was Captain Edward Tyng, and both praised him without reservation. A few days later one of the British sloops was sent off to London with dispatches, and Tyng was mentioned in them so prominently that he was the first member of the entire Louisburg expedition to win a special commendation from the Crown. King George II, acting on the advice of the Admiralty, granted him a permanent commission as a Captain in the Royal Navy, an unprecedented honor. He held the rank for the rest of his long life.

The weather had cleared by the time the frigates and sloops reached Louisburg, and Captain Robertson broke out the *Eltham's* signal flags to pass the good news to Commodore Warren and General Pepperrell. Word of the triumph spread rapidly, the guns of the *Vigilant* boomed a salute, and the militiamen on the plain south of the Citadel literally danced with joy.

But Louisburg, grim and forbidding, continued to hold out into the second week of June. In the wild excitement of the moment, few could forget that the final victory had not yet been attained.

12

The defeat of Colonel Marin and the Micmac ended the hostility between General Pepperrell and Commodore Warren. Their tensions lessened, the futile and expensive assault on the Island Battery was forgotten, and each was lavish in his praise of the accomplishments of the other's subordinates in the Battle of the Strait. Thereafter, for the rest of the siege, the two commanders worked closely together, in complete harmony. For the first time they formed a genuine personal friendship that would last as long as both men lived.

Their most immediate problem was not a military one, as such. Admiral du Chambon, they knew, was relying heavily on the relief he expected from Colonel Marin. Therefore they deemed it essential that he be notified he could expect no help from either French troops or their Indian allies. Obviously, he would not accept their word that a battle had taken place and that Marin had been defeated. Equally unhappily, General Waldo had taken no prisoners in the engagement. So the commanders of the expedition had to do what they could with the prisoners previously captured.

They planned the move with great care. Commodore Warren arranged a victory dinner on board the *Vigilant* for all of the senior officers who had taken part in the fight. He dipped into his personal larder for such delicacies as minced mutton preserved in butter, dried raisins, and a West Indian fruit jam that he had kept stored in the coldest part of the forward hold.

Captain Maisonfort, the captured French commander of the *Vigilant*, was invited to attend the dinner, as were two members of his staff. Since the main topic of conversation at the meal was the victory over Marin, Captain Maisonfort heard all of the important details of the engagement. The joy of the victors was obvious as they toasted each other in wine supplied for the occasion by General Pepperrell, and it certainly must have been clear to the prisoner that his captors were not staging a mock celebration for his benefit.

Warren and Pepperrell allowed Maisonfort twenty-four hours to consider this latest turn of events. Then they invited him to dine with them again, alone. "The Frenchman," Sir Peter wrote in his log, "was much shaken by our triumph. Gen'l. P. and I sympathized with him, well knowing how we would feel if the situation were reversed and we found ourselves in his unfortunate position."

Pepperrell, in his journal, gave a more detailed account of the private dinner. Captain Maisonfort's spirits were low, as his captors had anticipated. Both expressed their hope that the defeat of Colonel Marin would bring peace to the New World in the near future. Louisburg, cut off from help, could not stand alone indefinitely. Sooner or later Admiral du Chambon would be forced to surrender. How much better it would be if he gave in quickly, saving further bloodshed and misery on both sides.

Maisonfort agreed with Warren and Pepperrell that the French no longer could hope to win the campaign, and that Du Chambon would be wise to cut short the agonies on both sides by raising the white flag.

Once Maisonfort had expressed his own opinion, Pepperrell and Warren advanced the arguments they had prepared. The French officer, they said, could take an active, honorable part in hastening the peace negotiations. Carefully refraining from making further references to the Battle of the Strait, they suggested that they send Maisonfort into Louisburg on parole to discuss the situation with the French commandant.

Captain Maisonfort eagerly accepted the offer. He was granted a parole of thirty-six hours and was sent into the Citadel under a flag of truce. Until he returned, Pepperrell and Warren told him, their guns would remain silent. The order was given to every military and naval unit, and it was made clear that any man who broke the voluntary armistice would be subjected to severe punishment.

The members of the British and American high command waited in a torment of suspense. Maisonfort, they believed, would be certain to bring up the subject of Colonel Marin's defeat. Admiral du Chambon would then recognize the hard truth of his hopeless situation, and the great fortress would surrender.

Three hours before the end of the parole deadline, Captain Maisonfort rode out of the main south gate of the Citadel, accompanied by a small cavalry escort. General Pepperrell and Commodore Warren rode forward to meet him, their aides behind them. Amenities were exchanged, and the French officer in command of the cavalry detail was invited to Pepperrell's tent for a glass of wine. The offer was regretfully declined.

Maisonfort changed to a horse that Pepperrell had brought with him for the purpose, and the mount he had ridden out of Louisburg returned to the Citadel with the escort. The huge gates closed again.

Not until the three men reached General Pepperrell's tent did the crestfallen Maisonfort tell his story of what had happened. When he had first mentioned the Battle of the Strait, Admiral du Chambon had refused to believe him; in fact, Maisonfort said, he had been directly accused of being a traitor to France. Only after he challenged Du Chambon to a duel did the Admiral accept his word.

As Warren and Pepperrell had anticipated, the news of the Battle of the Strait was a crushing blow to the French.

Admiral du Chambon spent long hours in private conference with his own staff, and then told Maisonfort he could not seriously contemplate the idea of surrendering. His own reputation and the honor of France were at stake, he said. His troops were in good health, stocks of provisions and gunpowder were ample, and the morale of the garrison had been excellent ever since the assault on the Island Battery had been repulsed.

Du Chambon, Maisonfort informed his captors, had no intention of allowing his troops or the civilians of Louisburg to find out that the eagerly awaited reinforcements had been driven off. The few staff members who had been told the news had been sworn to secrecy.

The siege would continue. Eventually, Admiral du Chambon was convinced, the British and their colonials would become weary of sitting outside the walls of an impregnable fortress, and would go home. Although it would have been helpful had Marin arrived with his regiments and the Micmac, Du Chambon was prepared to wait out the campaign singlehanded. Louisburg has been built to stand alone for years, if necessary.

Du Chambon sent a brief verbal message to Commodore Warren and General Pepperrell. "Gentlemen," he told them, "you well may feel you have spent a long time on Cape Breton Island. But only the first chapter of our story has been written. I shall sit safely behind my walls for months to come, for years, if I must."

The artillery bombardment of Louisburg was resumed. From dawn until nightfall, the guns on the plain south of the fortress bombarded the Citadel, and the cannon in the Grand Battery and the Royal Battery pounded the solid rock of the Island Battery. Everything was as it had been prior to the Battle of the Strait, and the winners of that engagement lost their sense of exhilaration.

The basic situation remained unchanged. The Island Battery was still the key to Louisburg, and the high command agreed that only artillery could reduce it. In an attempt to reach it from a better vantage point, the Rhode Islanders moved some of their guns to a cliff that stood at right angles to the Royal Battery. Because of the position's height, it was possible to train guns more accurately on the target. By the same token, however, the gunners were more vulnerable to a counterattack by the Island Battery's cannoneers.

Colonel Hanscomb and Lieutenant Colonel Richard Gridley of the artillery worked miracles in moving heavy cannon up the steep side of the cliff. Gridley, who more than a quarter of a century later was an artillery officer in the Battle of Bunker Hill during the American Revolution, also worked out a method of hauling large boulders to the top of the cliff. The guns were emplaced behind this rough shield, which protected both the cannon and their crews.

One morning at low tide, a gunner, whose name has been lost to posterity, sat on the cliff, staring down into the water below. He thought he detected a number of heavy bronze cannon beneath the surface, and called out to his companions in wild excitement. Before noon a difficult salvage operation was initiated under Colonel Gridley's direction. The services of several hundred infantrymen and sailors were commandeered, and the men worked around the clock for two days and nights.

Their efforts yielded a prize as great as it was unexpected. In all, ten bronze cannon were recovered from the sea, each of them a mammoth twenty-four-pounder. The barnacles were scraped off, the guns were dried, and Colonel Hanscomb pronounced them in perfect condition.

Captain Maisonfort was familiar with the story of the cannon. They had fallen into the sea a decade earlier when a ship carrying them had foundered on the rocks, he said. Since that time the authorities at Louisburg had been aware of their presence just off the shore, but had felt that too much labor would be required to raise them.

The carelessness of the French paid great dividends to the Rhode Island gunners. The recovered cannon vastly increased the strength of the American artillery, and the Island Battery was subjected to a constant, heavy barrage.

By now the aim of the gunners had become superb. Long practice had enabled the Rhode Islanders to put their shot precisely where they wished, and the men of various batteries joked about their prowess. Their boasts gave Colonel Hanscomb an idea. If they were such experts, he wanted to know, were they capable of dropping howitzer shots onto cannon emplaced inside the Island Battery?

The gunners responded to the challenge at once, and the six-pounder howitzers, sometimes called mortars, were loaded with iron balls that were immersed in fire until they became red-hot. Four howitzers were fired in quick succession, and crews of two saw their shots sail into open gunports. An instant later twin explosions seemed to shake the entire area. The heated iron balls had landed on the French cannon, which had been torn apart when their own gunpower discharged.

One of the explosions was so savage that it tore away a chunk of the Island Battery's rock face. The astonished Rhode Islanders watched in horror as several wounded French gunners leaped to their death in the sea far below in an attempt to escape from an inferno created by still-exploding bags of gunpowder.

It seemed incredible that any cannoneers could have displayed such pin-point accuracy. But there were so many witnesses who wrote almost identical accounts of the incident that it had to be believed. Naval gunners on board the frigates applauded the artillerymen, as did scores of other Rhode Islanders stationed at the Grand Battery and the Royal Battery.

"Our gunners," a jubilant William Pepperrell wrote in his journal, "have demonstrated to the French that the Island Battery is not impregnable. A little group of colonials from Rhode Island have made a liar of Admiral du Chambon."

Plans could now be made for a new kind of bombardment, and Colonel Gridley was assigned the task of converting a number of twelve-pounder guns into mortars. This he achieved by elevating the muzzles after placing the guns on reinforced platforms. The cannon were not really howitzers, of course, but when loaded with a limited charge of gunpowder, could have the same effect. Heated shot of considerable size now could be lobbed through the air instead of being driven on a more direct line.

Colonel Hanscomb and Colonel Gridley reported to General Pepperrell that they believed they would be able to render the Island Battery useless.

Members of the high command joined the Rhode Island gunners on the cliff early the next morning. Excitement ran high. If six-pounder mortars had been able to create such havoc, what would twelve-pounders do?

The answer to the question had to be delayed. Someone called Commodore Warren's attention to the presence of several sails in the distance, and Sir Peter immediately descended the cliff and had himself rowed out to the *Vigilant* in his gig. Long before he reached his flagship the entire squadron had been alerted, and seamen were at their battle stations.

Generals Pepperrell and Waldo watched the ensuing drama from the vantage point of the cliff. Five ships were sailing toward Louisburg, and one of the Rhode Island gunners, who was a Newport fisherman in civilian life, identified them as merchantmen. When they drew closer he was proved correct. All were brigs, and all defiantly raised the lily-ensign of France to their topgallants.

Apparently their masters had been misinformed about the situation at Louisburg. The merchant ships sailed directly toward the harbor entrance, obviously believing that the Royal and Grand Batteries were still in French hands. Equally evident was the newcomers' ignorance of the size and strength of the combined British and American colonial fighting squadron.

Commodore Warren waited until the slow, cumbersome brigs were too close to escape, and then gave chase. His sloops of war skimmed over the water, firing shots across the bows of the brigs, and when the frigates followed, ready for action, the masters of the merchant vessels were forced to surrender.

All five of the vessels were heavily laden with food, rum, and brandywine from the French West Indian Islands. In fact, there was sufficient food and more than enough liquor in their holds to supply the invaders' needs for weeks to come.

The crews of the brigs were taken prisoner, and their masters were questioned by a curious Commodore Warren. They told him they had been sent to Louisburg from Martinique, and they had indeed been given false information. The Governor of the French West Indian Islands had informed them that a British land force had invaded Cape Breton Island and was investing Louisburg. But no mention had been made of the capture of the key artillery points at the entrance to the harbor. Similarly, the brigs' masters had been told that most of the ships carrying the investing force to Louisburg had been driven off by a French squadron headed by the *Vigilant*.

The brigs' masters had recognized the silhouette of the *Vigilant* from a considerable distance. Believing the information they had been given to be accurate, they had continued on their course, not discovering their mistake until too late.

Undoubtedly Admiral du Chambon had seen the sea drama from the towers of the Citadel. Both Pepperrell and Warren were able to imagine how he felt. "I know," Sir Peter wrote in his log, "that poor Du Chambon must regret the boasts he made to us through Maisonfort. Thanks to the stupidity of his colleagues in the West Indian Islands, we shall eat heartily, whilst he must dig deeper into his moldering stores of flour and cornmeal and salt fish."

Not until late afternoon was the capture of the brigs brought to a successful completion. Then the attention of the high command reverted to Colonel Gridley and the Rhode Island gunners. The twelve-pounder "howitzers" were fired, and by the second round the cannoneers found their targets. Shot after shot dropped into the open gunports of the Island Battery.

The explosions that followed were deafening, and the men on the cliff were stunned by the results of their efforts. Huge chunks of the supposedly invulnerable rock that housed the French soldiers and guns of the Island Battery were torn away, leaving gaping holes. Whole sections of cannon platform were exposed, as were connecting tunnels and other interior chambers.

Bodies of French defenders littered the platforms, where smoke continued to curl up into the air from the ruins of twisted metal. None of the Englishmen or Americans on the platform cheered, though they had succeeded in breaking open the door to Louisburg. The devastation was too great.

"I felt ill," Colonel Hanscomb wrote to his wife. "So great was the loss and life and damage, that I could eat no supper that night, nor breakfast the next morning. I knew our work was not yet complete and the contemplation of the dreadful task still ahead caused me to cringe."

The coming of night forced a postponement of further operations until morning. General Pepperrell and Commodore Warren dined together that evening on provisions taken from the French brigs, but neither had any appetite, and the atmosphere was gloomy. The goal they had envisioned from the time the expedition to Louisburg had first been planned was at last within reach. But the prospect of carnage and destruction took the edge off their enthusiasm.

Soon after dawn on the morning of June 15, the Rhode Island gun crews went to work again. The twelve-pounders that were being used as mortars continued to drop heated shot into the gunports of the Island Battery, and section after section of rock was ripped away. "By noon," Pepperrell noted in his journal, "Gridley estimated that more than one hundred French cannoneers had been slaughtered."

Scores of militia officers and men who had nothing else to occupy them gathered on the cliff to watch the grisly spectacle. Like those who had seen the previous day's destruction, they remained silent through the entire operation. The principles of chivalry that had been in vogue since the Middle Ages had not yet been abandoned, and these eighteenth-century soldiers were shocked by the brutality of what they and their comrades were doing.

"Our work was necessary," Hanscomb said in his letter to his wife. "By crushing the artillerymen in the Island Battery and rendering it inoperable, we were shortening the campaign. So, overall, we reduced the casualties that both sides would suffer. But it was difficult to think in terms of the future when the shattered walls of the great rock ran red with the blood of our foes."

The French were not content to remain passively on the defensive, and struck back with desperate fury. Although at least half of the Island Battery's guns had been knocked out of commission by noon, stunning the defenders, the French gunners retaliated as best they could. They returned the bombardment with the most effective cannon at their disposal, their thirteen-pounder howitzers and their fourteen-pounder bronze guns, which were known as sakers.

Not until late morning did they find the range. Then they made the Rhode Islanders' attack expensive. Three of the American guns were destroyed, and so many enemy shots landed on the cliff that more than thirty of the spectators were killed or wounded. The rest wisely dispersed.

Hanscomb and Gridley, crouching behind the boulders that formed a crude defensive shield, realized that in spite of the damage they were causing, the French could inflict equal damage unless the pace of the assault were stepped up. Therefore they ordered their twenty-four-pounders, including the ten guns taken from the sea, to be put into action.

These huge artillery pieces opened their bombardment with a salvo of such severity that men a half mile from the scene claimed they could feel the impact. "The very ground beneath our feet trembled," a militiaman from Boston wrote to his family, "and we were afraid the earth might open and swallow us up."

The French, valiantly trying to maintain their positions, clung desperately to the Island Battery. While the twenty-four-pounders were laying down a heavy barrage it was impossible for them to return the enemy's fire. "So intense was the fire of the British colonials," wrote Captain Louis d'Aillebout, commander of the Island Battery, in his report to Admiral du Chambon, "that no man could stand. We pressed our faces against the stone flooring of the cells we occupied, each praying to God that he would be spared."

The twenty-four-pounders continued to thunder for the better part of the afternoon. The cannon became so hot that younger crew members were ordered to lower buckets into the sea on long lines, and to throw the water onto the barrels of the guns to cool them. Cannoneers were deafened by the steady roar, and it became necessary to give orders with hand signals. The hearing of at least five of the Rhode Islanders was permanently impaired, according to Colonel Hanscomb.

Two hours before sunset the fire of the twenty-four-pounders slackened, and the howitzers went to work again. The internal structure of the fort had been increasingly weakened by the heavy bombardment, and through jagged holes in the rock the Rhode Islanders could actually see sections of the honeycombed cavern crumbling away. "I do not believe it possible," Hanscomb said in a hastily scribbled note to General Pepperrell, "for the enemy to maintain organized resistance much longer."

The corps commander held a hasty conference with Commodore Warren, and it was agreed that the ships of the squadron were better equipped than the militiamen to take full advantage of the situation that might develop. Three of the frigates and several sloops were ordered to maintain alert stations at the entrance to the harbor.

The end came swiftly. One of the twelve-pounder mortars in a two-gun battery commanded by Lieutenant Abraham Martin of Providence, Rhode Island, sent a glowing iron ball high into the air. It crashed down through the weakened flooring of the interior of the stone fort. Still red-hot, it penetrated the powder magazine of the Island Battery, which exploded.

The tremendous detonation knocked everyone on the cliff from his feet. A young infantryman from New Jersey stationed on the plain south of the Citadel wrote to his fiancée, "I thought that the end of the world had come."

Firing was immediately suspended.

Flames could be seen leaping into the air from the inside of the Island Battery, and the men on the cliff wondered whether any of the defenders were still alive. It was impossible to imagine a man surviving the terrible explosion.

But thirty or forty of the French artillerymen were uninjured, although dazed by the blast. Among them was Captain d'Aillebout, who knew that he and his men had reached the limits of their endurance. His flagstaff and the banner of French lilies flying from it had been swept away earlier in the day during the bombardment by the twenty-four-pounders, so he could not lower his colors. Instead he ripped off his sweat-soaked white silk shirt, moved to one of the holes in the rock, and waved the garment as a signal of surrender.

The waiting frigates and sloops immediately sailed across the bay, tacking frequently to avoid the cannon-ading from the Citadel, which stood behind the Island Battery. Then, protected by the hulk of the shattered fort, they anchored close to the shore, and Royal Marines quickly occupied the key to Louisburg. Captain d'Aillebout and the surviving members of his garrison were accorded full honors of war, and the gallant commander of the Island Battery was entertained that night at dinner by Pepperrell, Warren, and Hanscomb.

Colonel Gridley was too busy to attend the affair. All through the long night, weary Rhode Island gunners moved howitzers and some of their heavier cannon into the ruined fort. Now they were so close to the Citadel that rifle and musket shots could cut down men on the inner bastion's sentry platforms. So it was obvious that cannon would do great damage to buildings inside the walls.

"We have taken the Island Battery, at long last," Sir Peter Warren noted in his log. "After anticipating this day for so long, it is difficult for General P., as it is for me, to realize that the great day has arrived. Louisburg can no longer hold out against us. If du Chambon were not a stubborn Frenchman who has more pride than common sense, he would surrender the Citadel to us at once. Alas! He entertains such fears of his monarch, the tyrant of Versailles, that he does not dare raise the white ensign until all hope is gone.

"French troops will surely die in the days ahead. It grieves me to think that the men and women of Louisburg who have taken refuge behind the walls of the Citadel will also suffer mortal danger. But their ordeal cannot be a long one. We have shown that any fort built by man can be captured by man, so the last victory is within sight. We intend to take the Citadel as rapidly as our skills and courage permit."

13

Louisburg was now at the mercy of the invaders' artillery. The frigates and sloops of Sir Peter Warren's squadron, anchored close to the inner shore of the harbor, lobbed heated cannonballs over the walls of the Citadel. The howitzers of the Rhode Islanders, precariously emplaced in the hulk of the Island Battery, did the same.

The new bombardment began at dawn on the morning of June 16, and continued all day, every day, without a pause. The French had only one cause for comfort. The attackers were now too close to the Citadel for their larger cannon to be effective. The twenty-four-pounders of the land-based artillery could not be elevated sufficiently so that their shot would clear the walls, nor could the larger guns on the warships.

The heavier cannon continued to fire, of course, chipping away at the masonry of the thick walls. But it was the mortars that did the real damage. Wanting to end the campaign as quickly and with as little loss of life as possible, General Pepperrell and Commodore Warren called a meeting of all officers, both military and naval. Pepperrell made a brief speech.

Ordinarily, he said, he was opposed to the use of "grape" as an uncivilized weapon of war, although both sides already had used it on a limited scale. But the sooner the French could be made to realize their situation was hopeless, the sooner Admiral du Chambon would surrender. Therefore he suggested that, in addition to heated shot, the mortars fire grape over the walls. Both he and

Warren believed, he declared, that the officers should be given a voice in the matter. If they hesitated or were unwilling to commit themselves, he and Sir Peter would not shrink from their responsibilities as commanders, and would give the artillery orders to use the metal fragments as ammunition. If, on the other hand, a majority of the officers voted against the use of grape, the commanders would be bound by their decision.

Warren, Pepperrell, and General Waldo left the meeting so that they would not influence the balloting. Captain Robertson of the *Eltham* acted as chairman, and called for a free, open discussion. Colonel Vaughan subsequently wrote a short, moving pamphlet entitled, *The Art of War* in which he described the scene that followed.

"Two score officers clamored for recognition from the chair," he wrote. "Speaker after speaker, officer after officer, approved the use of langrage (grape). Then the dissenters voiced their opinions. I found it odd in the extreme that the only gentlemen present who were strongly opposed to the use of this barbaric ammunition were artillery officers. The gunnery officers of our own and the Royal frigates, together with the militia gunnery officers, stood together in their condemnation. None was more eloquent than Tom Hanscomb, who offered a motion against the suggestion made by our commander in chief. He was seconded in this endeavor by the most ferocious sailor in Massachusetts Bay, Lieutenant Nehemiah Allen, First Lieutenant and Director of Gunnery to Captain Edward Tyng."

Only the artillerymen, it seemed, were aware of the devastating effect of grape on an enemy. And only the artillerymen voted in favor of Colonel Hanscomb's motion. The other officers unanimously endorsed the suggestion of General Pepperrell and Commodore Warren. The corps acted accordingly.

All militiamen who had been blacksmiths in civilian life were excused from other duty. These men were put to work breaking up scrap iron and other metal into small pieces. They labored so energetically that the first grape was sent over the Citadel's walls by the Rhode Island howitzers that same day. The siege had entered a new stage.

The suffering of both civilians and soldiers inside the Citadel was intense. Heated shot set fire to houses and other buildings not made of stone, and it soon became impossible for anyone to walk through the streets and compounds of the great fort without risking sudden death or serious injury. Admiral du Chambon was forced to order all noncombatants to move into the shelter of thick-ceilinged, stone-walled barracks. Fighting men, of course, continued to take their chances.

François Bigot, the Intendant, or second in command, had been keeping a diary for some months, and now expanded his observations in its pages. "Lest others and I be called derelict in our devotion to the Motherland," he wrote candidly, "I am keeping this account of our travail."

Few members of the garrison held out real hope that Louisburg could stand firm indefinitely. Only Admiral du Chambon, Bigot declared, professed to be optimistic. But even he privately admitted to the Intendant that the pressures were becoming unbearable. The roar of militia and Royal Navy cannon kept everyone indoors from daybreak until sundown. Sentries were reluctant to walk on the platforms behind the walls that faced the Island Battery and the harbor. Two Swiss mercenaries, men who had spent years in French service, climbed over the wall looking out on the south plain one night, and deserted to the enemy.

The following night three more Swiss did the same. Thereafter all members of the Swiss contingent, more than one hundred and fifty men in all, were given no active-duty assignments, but were ordered to remain in their quarters. There they were kept under watch, none too diplomatically, by French troops armed with loaded muskets and bayonets. The Swiss resented this treatment, and became so insulting that several fights broke out between them and their guards.

"The disturbances," Bigot said in his diary, "were at first believed to be an insurrection. But I am inclined toward the view that the majority of the Swiss mercenaries are honorable men who have no intention of breaking their vow to fight in the service of King Louis."

Groping for patches of brightness in the gloom, the Intendant wrote that the policy of keeping everyone indoors was holding casualties to a minimum. "No civilians have been killed since the enemy began using langrage extensively," he wrote on June 19. "It is true that two foolish citizens were wounded, but the fault was their own, since they disobeyed the order to remain within safe shelter during daylight hours."

Early on the morning of June 20, a number of sails were sighted on the horizon by lookouts on both sides. The French, counting the sails of seven ships and watching Commodore Warren's seamen prepare for battle, dared to hope that real relief was at last on its way. But they suffered the pangs of fresh disappointment when they saw the ship in the van raise the Union Jack.

"The arrival of reinforcements is a miraculous coincidence that will shatter the last, dying hopes of the French," Commodore Warren wrote in his log, and he was right.

The Royal Navy had dispatched four frigates and three sloops of war to assist in the blockade of Louisburg. The larger vessels, the *Princess Mary, Canterbury, Chester,* and *Hector,* each mounted forty-four guns. The three sloops were of the latest design, and no ships on the high seas were faster or could maneuver with greater agility.

Warren's squadron had expanded to the status of a fleet. Now he was strong enough to meet any challenge at sea that the admirals in Paris cared to offer him. And the noose choking Louisburg was pulled a notch tighter.

The final deterioration of the situation within the Citadel occurred later that day, or perhaps that night. Admiral du Chambon was imprecise as to the time in his report to King Louis, and Bigot was equally vague in his diary. But the facts were clear enough. A munitions officer named Le Brun, who went to the ammunition cellars deep below the surface of the earth, made a shocking discovery.

Vaults that supposedly contained gunpowder were filled instead with bags of flour piled from stone floor to stone ceiling.

Admiral du Chambon hurried to the vault, lantern in hand, to see for himself what had happened. He and Bigot made personal inspections of all supplies on hand, and before daybreak the next morning had convinced themselves that the worst was true. For months they had fooled themselves, believing Louisburg had enough powder to last for at least another year. That belief was based on false information.

Perhaps a previous governor or one of his subordinates had removed gunpowder, selling it for personal profit and substituting flour for it in the vault. Perhaps a munitions officer had made an honest but stupid error when the powder on hand had been counted. Whatever the reason, Louisburg was almost bankrupt.

Even if powder were used sparingly, the supply would be exhausted within a few weeks. The Citadel's ability to retaliate when attacked would soon cease to exist.

Trumpeters awakened officers, soldiers, and civilians in every part of the Citadel to read them a short, bitter proclamation that Admiral du Chambon had scribbled on a torn piece of paper. "Our gunpowder has reached the vanishing point, and we have lost the ability to wage war. The circumstances offer me no alternative to the unhappy course I must take. Long live France!"

At daybreak, the Rhode Islanders in the Island Battery and on the south plain were preparing to resume their bombardment of the Citadel, as were the gunners on the many warships clustered at the inner side of the harbor. Suddenly the unexpected roll of drums was heard from the parapets of the great fort. Aides ran into General Pepperrell's tent to summon him, and Commodore Warren was interrupted at his breakfast table on board the *Vigilant*.

The two commanders, from their separate vantage points, peered through the early morning haze as a white flag was hoisted to the top of the pole above the Citadel's central ramparts.

Pepperrell immediately ordered all units to suspend their fire. Warren, separately, gave the same command to the gunners on board the frigates. Then, in such haste that he twisted his ankle as he stepped into his gig, Sir Peter came ashore to join his co-commander.

The two leaders of the expedition were together on the south plain when the main gate of Louisburg opened. A full troop of cavalry in dress uniforms escorted Admiral du Chambon's personal aide across the swampy flatland, the pennant bearer carrying another flag of truce. The message the young Frenchman delivered was brief and dramatic.

Admiral du Chambon was requesting an armistice, and wanted to know the British-American surrender terms.

Pepperrell, whose career as a successful merchant had accustomed him to the give and take of negotiating, became the spokesman for the invaders. What, he demanded was Du Chambon's offer? He and Sir Peter would wait twenty-four hours for detailed terms, he said. Thereafter, the British fleet and American colonial militiamen would terminate the armistice and launch a general assault on the Citadel if the offer proved inadequate.

Admiral du Chambon and Intendant Bigot worked all day and most of the night on their proposal. Trying to protect France, French property, and the persons of French subjects, they hedged their offer with numerous qualifications.

When Pepperrell and Warren read the document the following morning, there was no need for discussion. According to Colonel Vaughan, who was present on the south plain, they merely glanced at one another. "The General," Vaughan wrote to his wife, "replied to the aide of Governor du Chambon that we insisted on the unconditional surrender of the garrison. The French were given four hours, until twelve o'clock, noon, to agree. In order to prove that we meant what we said, all troops and ships were ordered to prepare for immediate resumption of hostilities."

Du Chambon saw the militiamen lashing together their scaling ladders, and watched the frigates preparing for action. He was trapped, and knew it. Having admitted to the enemy that he was no longer capable of continuing the struggle against them, he had lost his ability to maneuver. Retiring to his private office, he slowly composed a new communication.

"Gentlemen," he wrote, "my honor compels me to refuse your demand that I surrender without condition. Grant me but one right, however, and I shall agree to any other terms you see fit to impose upon me. My duty to His Christian Majesty, Louis, forces me to insist that my troops be permitted to march out of the Citadel carrying their arms and colors."

The attempt to salvage what little he could of his pride was so pathetic that Pepperrell and Warren agreed to the request. Their other surrender terms, which they drew up at once, were firm but fair. They insisted that French military personnel evacuate Louisburg, and that all armaments, gunpowder, and cannon be handed over to the victors. They demanded that every member of the garrison pledge that he would not take up arms against

Great Britain or her colonies within the next twelve months, and that all British and American colonial prisoners of war be returned immediately.

The final demand was uncompromising: the Citadel was to be handed over to Commodore Warren and General Pepperrell no later than six o'clock that same evening.

In return, the conquerors were generous. All French officers and civilians who wished to live in the town of Louisburg would be permitted to dwell there, without molestation, and to engage in whatever religious practices they saw fit. No eighteenth-century people were more conscious of the principles of religious freedom than Americans and Englishmen.

Officers who had no desire to remain in Louisburg would be given transportation to Quebec on board British warships. Noncommissioned officers and soldiers, however, would board the troop transports and remain there under guard until arrangements could be made to take them to France. And all French wounded and sick would be given the same medical care afforded members of the victorious expedition.

Pepperrell and Warren were also generous to Admiral du Chambon, the members of his staff, and Intendant Bigot. All would be returned to France, if they wished, on board British warships, which would supply them with any provisions they needed on the voyage. As a courteous gesture, Du Chambon was also granted the right to take two wagonloads of personal belongings from Louisburg. Both wagons could be covered, so that no one would know what property he was taking, and the baggage would be subject only to the inspection of one officer, who would insure that he was transporting "no warlike stores."

A final offer was cryptic: "If there are any persons in the town or garrison whom you shall desire not to be seen by us, they shall be permitted to go off masked." In other words, French espionage agents would have the right to conceal their identity! That same day, Colonel Vaughan wrote his wife, three masked men were permitted to leave the Citadel, and were last seen heading into the interior wilderness of Cape Breton Island.

The articles were signed by the opposing commanders, and late in the afternoon of June 22, the French garrison marched out, the troops carrying their muskets, which they later relinquished. French officers were permitted to keep their swords.

A French band played, and a fife and drum corps from New York replied. Intendant Bigot carried the gilded keys to the fort, symbols of possession of Louisburg, and presented one to General Pepperrell, one to Commodore Warren.

Strict decorum was observed on both sides, and the British sailors and American soldiers were warned that any man who intimidated the Louisburg civilians would be tried by a court-martial board and would be subject to a long term in prison. The civilians were already returning to their homes in the town, and were astonished to find that none of their property had been stolen.

Nothing prevented the troops and seamen from taking "souvenirs" out of the Citadel, however, and the long corridors of the fort were quickly stripped of their ornaments. A number of officers found paintings and other valuable property in the official apartments of the higher-ranking Frenchmen, and these, too, quickly vanished.

Admiral du Chambon was taken on board the *Vigilant*, where he was given temporary quarters, and the members of his staff went off to various frigates. The Union Jack was hoisted over the ramparts, and at nine o'clock on the evening of June 22, General Pepperrell, who had taken possession of the fortress, gave a banquet for Commodore Warren and the officers of both military and naval forces. The food was hastily prepared, to be sure, and the meal was no different than that served the officers on any other night, but large quantities of brandywine and rum were made available, so the occasion was an unqualified success.

When the officers looked out at the ramparts, they saw sentries from New England, the central colonies, Maryland, and Virginia marching up and down the platforms. That fact, far more than the conviviality of the banquet, gave them cause for rejoicing. Louisburg, the most powerful fort ever built in the New World, had been captured by militiamen, colonial sailors, and a small squadron of Royal Navy ships.

The wild scheme initiated in Boston had become reality, and the news of Louisburg's fall would stun the entire civilized world.

14

The conquerors of Louisburg had little opportunity to savor their accomplishments. Their victory had been a magnificent achievement, but it could be reversed at any time. The war was still raging, and the officers who were responsible for the capture of the great fortress felt certain that France would make a supreme effort to regain control of the bastion that had been the symbol of her power in the New World.

Less than a week after the Citadel had been taken, the masters of New England fishing boats who put into the harbor brought with them rumors of impending disaster. The most common of the stories was that an exceptionally strong corps of six thousand professional soldiers was being organized at Quebec for the purpose of conducting a countersiege. It was reported that every garrison and post in New France was being denuded of its troops for the purpose, and that an urgent appeal had been sent to Paris for reinforcements.

A sloop of war arriving from England with dispatches brought equally alarming information. On the very day that Louisburg had fallen, the strongest French fleet assembled since the start of the war had put out of Brest. Commanded by the Duc d'Anville, the ablest and most energetic admiral in the French navy, it had consisted of at least six ships of the line and eleven frigates, as well as an even larger number of smaller vessels.

In spite of its size, this fleet had managed to elude the British warships trying to maintain a blockade of the

French coast, and had last been seen sailing in the direction of Cape Breton Island. Commodore Warren was forced to assume, therefore, that D'Anville had been sent to relieve Louisburg. He ordered his ships to maintain a constant alert, and sent several sloops of war ranging far into the Atlantic to maintain a watch for the enemy. The threat never materialized, however, as D'Anville's fleet was scattered by severe storms.

The militiamen were given little chance to celebrate their victory, either. No sooner had they settled down in the barracks of the Citadel than they were ordered to start repairing the damage they themselves had wrought. Every member of the expeditionary force who was not sick or wounded was put to work.

Most of the stone that had been used in the original construction of the fort was to be found on the north shore of Cape Breton Island. General Pepperrell needed vast quantities of it for repair purposes, so Commodore Warren assigned three of his ships to transport it to Louisburg after soldiers, most of them masons in civilian life, had cut it into appropriate blocks.

The artillerymen in particular resented the efforts of the high command to force them to rebuild some of the walls they themselves had damaged. But there was no choice. The besiegers might themselves be besieged at any time, and even the worst grumblers knew their survival might depend on the success of their reconstruction efforts.

A number of significant changes were made in the defense works. General Pepperrell was concerned because of the relative ease with which the militiamen had captured the Grand and Royal Batteries. What Americans had done might be repeated by the French. So both of the miniature forts were torn down. Colonel Gridley drew plans for a new and stronger post, and construction was begun on the heights of the cliff. A single, strong fort that really dominated the entrance to the harbor was preferable to two smaller, vulnerable posts, Warren and Pepperrell agreed.

The Island Battery caused the greatest problems. It had been virtually demolished by Rhode Island artillerymen, and had been rendered useless. The first task was to clear away vast amounts of rubble, and reduce what was left of the original rock shell to its foundations. Then a completely new artillery post would have to be constructed on the site. It was obvious that a project of this magnitude would take a long time to complete, and the work could not be rushed. The officers in charge did their best, but progress was slow.

While the soldiers and seamen at Cape Breton Island continued to labor, news of the victory was carried by two of Commodore Warren's fastest sloops to Boston and London. In both the New World and the Old, word of the victory had an electrifying effect. Governor Shirley declared a public holiday in Massachusetts Bay, and the governors of other colonies followed his example. In every city and town of consequence, people celebrated with torchlight parades, the burning of bonfires, and noisy barbecue suppers at which all citizens were welcome.

In England, the capture of Louisburg was hailed as a military event of the greatest significance. William Pitt said in a House of Commons speech that English domination of North America was assured, and that, no matter what the outcome of the war elsewhere, the French had lost their secure hold on Canada.

Equally important was the effect on the war being waged in Europe. Ever since the time of Henry IV, at the beginning of the seventeenth century, France had been the most powerful military force in the Old World. Her armies had been respected and feared everywhere. A few thousand American colonials and British seamen changed that image overnight. The prestige of France declined immediately. Pitt and others later attributed the ultimate

British victory, won in 1748, at least partly to the loss in stature suffered by France when Louisburg fell.

Great Britain rewarded the conquerors with deserved generosity. Commodore Warren was promoted, and as Rear Admiral Warren he was given seniority over more than fifty percent of his peers. General Pepperrell was made a baronet, a hereditary form of knighthood, and thereafter was called Sir William. He was the first native-born American ever to be accorded such an honor by the Crown. He was also made the colonel of a regiment in the Regular Army.

This appointment was more than an empty honor. Under the military system operating in the eighteenth century, permanent commissions were purchased by those who had the funds as well as the necessary professional requisites for the posts. The income from these sales was split by the Crown and the regimental commander. A colonel, who rarely accompanied his regiment into the field, held his position for life, and hence was assured of a steady source of income.

Governor Shirley was also given a Regular Army regiment, and, if he chose, was entitled to be addressed by his military title. Shirley estimated that the honor was worth an income of five hundred pounds per year, the equivalent of more than five thousand dollars two centuries later.

The colonies, too, were unstinting in their rewards. Pepperrell, Waldo, and the commanders of regiments were confirmed in their ranks for the rest of their days, even if they retired from active military service. And Admiral Warren was given a sizable tract of land on the Massachusetts Bay frontier. He did not use it himself, but a decade later was able to sell it for a large sum.

Meanwhile, the preparations to defend Louisburg in the event of a French counterattack continued. About a month after the capture of the fortress, one of the British sloops that had been standing out to sea on patrol duty returned with word that a number of French ships were approaching Cape Breton Island. These vessels were not part of the Duc d'Anville's fleet, however, but were merchantmen, escorted by a single French navy frigate. They were sailing from the south rather than the east, so it was assumed they were coming from the French West Indian Islands.

Warren had ample power to destroy the one French warship, but, in order to avoid unnecessary bloodshed, preferred to use guile. Pepperrell cooperated with him, and French flags were hoisted over the Citadel. Warren's ships anchored in the harbor, just inside the entrance, and when the enemy convoy appeared, its leaders assumed that the siege had ended with Louisburg still in French hands.

The frigate led the merchantmen into the harbor, and Warren closed the trap. Several of his frigates quickly blocked the entrance, and the others crowded the French frigate and merchantmen, making it impossible for the enemy to put up a fight. The entire convoy was forced to surrender.

In addition to cocoa and other produce from Martinique and the other French West Indian Islands, the convoy carried a vast fortune in gold and silver ingots and coins from Peru, most of it secured in the hold of the frigate. In all, the booty was worth the staggering sum of more than one million pounds.

One-half belonged to the Crown under British custom, and the rest went to the officers and crews of the Royal Navy and American colonial ships. Warren, whose personal share was known as "the Admiral's Eighth," was eventually awarded almost seventy thousand pounds. This included his profits from the *Vigilant* and the French brigs previously captured, and was the equivalent of nearly seven hundred thousand dollars in the latter part of the twentieth century.

British and American able-bodied seamen each received more than nine hundred pounds, and were thus well rewarded for their efforts throughout the siege. Militiamen and their officers did not share in the prize, which caused considerable dissatisfaction in the ranks of the troops who were working so hard to repair the defenses of Louisburg. Some units sent petitions of protest to General Pepperrell, but there was nothing he could do to win his men a share. The custom of the age remained inviolate.

Transports were made ready to take the sick and wounded back to Boston. Other men, perfectly healthy but bored by the tedious routine of garrison existence, also requested the right to return home. Their pleas were rejected, and the transports sailed with seven hundred soldiers on board.

However, Pepperrell knew there would be trouble if he ignored the demands of his troops. He sent a confidential letter to Governor Shirley, urging that replacements for his regiments and battalions be sent to Cape Breton Island as rapidly as they could be mustered.

Shirley, as always, responded promptly. The French were too busy making plans to recapture Louisburg to send Indian raiders to harass frontier settlers, so it was relatively easy to raise new units. About a month after the fall of the Citadel, one thousand men went to Louisburg from Massachusetts Bay and its Maine District, and, the following month another five hundred were sent by Rhode Island. By autumn New York, Connecticut, and Pennsylvania contributed another fifteen hundred, so no more than one thousand members of the original expedition were forced to remain at Louisburg.

The following year, Massachusetts Bay raised two more regiments, each of four hundred men, and subsequently the only veterans of the siege who stayed on were men who volunteered for such duty. Most were noncommissioned officers. By 1746 it became difficult to find troops willing to serve at the fort. Men stationed there had been writing home about the unpleasant existence they were forced to endure, and their description of their lot made others unwilling to replace them.

Life at the post was neither easy nor relaxed. The threat of a French counterattack, which never materialized, was always present, so the troops had to be on the alert at all times. The work of rebuilding the damaged fortifications was grueling, and soldiers worked sixty to seventy hours per week, exclusive of sentry duty. Almost inevitably, relations with the French civilians of the town of Louisburg deteriorated.

Most residents of the community returned to their former vocations, which consisted in the main of serving the garrison. "Never," wrote Captain Samuel Scales of Springfield, Massachusetts, "have I seen so many tailors and tavern keepers."

Sir William Pepperrell, who had assumed the duties of governor, tried valiantly, but in vain, to keep the peace. Soldiers insisted they were being charged too much for a drink of rum or the repair of their boots. Townsmen complained that the militiamen refused to pay them for legitimate services rendered. There were frequent fights over girls, too. The men of Louisburg naturally resented the attentions paid by the troops to their daughters and wives, while the militiamen, lonely and eager for feminine companionship, paid court to every attractive young woman in Louisburg. There were so many brawls in the autumn of 1745 that General Pepperrell restored peace only by threatening to declare the town out of bounds for his corps.

Illness plagued the militia during the winter of 1745-46. The air was always damp and raw, heavy snowfalls were frequent, and the bitter cold was unrelieved. Men who had become accustomed to out-of-door living were crowded together in cramped, poorly ventilated barracks, where sanitary facilities were inadequate. "When one man coughs," a corporal from Norwich, Connecticut, wrote to his mother, "fifty men fall ill with the ague."

Many became seriously incapacitated. There were few physicians serving with the corps, and their requests to Boston and Philadelphia for additional medicines and poultices were sometimes ignored. Not until Governor Shirley conducted a personal investigation of the matter was it discovered that a contractor in Boston had been stealing medical supplies prepared for shipment to Louisburg.

Men complained, too, of their monotonous diet of cornmeal, jerked beef, and salt fish. The supply masters could buy no produce from the farmers of Cape Breton Island during the winter months, and life became increasingly dreary.

Uniforms wore out, but the legislatures of Massachusetts Bay and other colonies, which had not yet been reimbursed by the Crown for their expenses, were reluctant to appropriate additional funds. General Pepperrell quietly solved the crisis by dipping into his personal fortune and buying cloth, leather for boots, and provisions through Thomas Hancock in Boston. In all, by the time he was relieved of his command, he had spent more than ten thousand pounds of his own money for his troops' food and clothing.

Within the next two years, the colonies themselves were repaid by the British government for the funds they had appropriated to prosecute the war. Pepperrell, however, never received a penny, although he sent several petitions to the Crown. He was a wealthy man who didn't need the money, but he remarked, on one occasion after the war, that "the cost of my baronetcy was rather high."

The discontent of the troops threatened to break out into open mutiny by the spring of 1746. Pepperrell sympathized with his men, and confided to General Waldo that he wouldn't blame them "if they should seek some means of altering their miserable condition."

The possibility of a French counterattack increased with the arrival of warmer weather, however, and Sir William could take no chances. Unwilling to write too much about the precarious morale of his men, he sent General Waldo to deliver a personal report to Governor Shirley.

As soon as he heard Waldo's report, Governor Shirley summoned the Massachusetts Bay Assembly into secret session. Not waiting for the legislators to gather from all over the colony, he appointed Thomas Hancock as his special representative, and ordered the merchant to fill the holds of three large brigs with venison, beef, and bacon, as well as potatoes, rice, and "such vegetables as will remain edible for a period of at least a fortnight."

When the Assembly convened, Governor Shirley bluntly repeated what he had been told by General Waldo, and after hearing him speak, the legislators voted the entire Louisburg garrison a raise in wages, retroactive to the day the Citadel had been taken. Armed with the weapons he believed he needed, Shirley sailed for Cape Breton Island in the convoy carrying the provisions.

The militiamen were so disgruntled that they offered no thanks when the food for which they had been longing was taken from the ships. In fact, a number of men made a point of remarking, in Governor Shirley's hearing, that such supplies were long overdue. But the atmosphere changed instantly when the entire garrison was mustered and General Pepperrell presented the Governor, who announced that the wages of each man were being doubled, going from one pound per month to two.

"There will be no mutiny," Sir William wrote to General Waldo, who had gone to the Maine District for a brief visit with his family before returning to Louisburg. "Today the men invited Shirley to dine with them in their garrison mess, an honor they have never accorded you or me. I marvel," he added, "at the fortitude of the troops we command. They gain no glory, they earn but a pittance, yet they serve faithfully and well. I cannot condemn them for their longing to return to the hearths of their loved ones."

Pepperrell, like his militiamen, was growing tired of foreign service. He, too, had been separated from his family for a long time. And, although he made no complaint, his many business interests were suffering because of his protracted absence from Massachusetts Bay. He remained a good soldier, however, and made no mention of his feelings when Governor Shirley sailed back to Boston.

Scouts and espionage agents who had traveled through New France and had visited Quebec brought word to Louisburg that the French had not yet been able to muster enough troops to launch a counterinvasion of Cape Breton Island. A shortage of manpower had always been a liability of the French in the New World. Now, on the defensive everywhere and afraid the British and Americans might try to capture Quebec itself, they were in no mood to conduct offensive operations.

The strong possibility remained, however, that an expedition might be sent from France to retake Louisburg, so sea and land patrols had to be maintained at all times. And from sunrise to sundown, six days each week, the militiamen continued to repair the damaged fortifications.

Pepperrell had discussed the idea of sending a strong corps to Quebec, but had agreed that Massachusetts Bay and her sister colonies could not afford the venture. They had not yet received repayment from England for their expenses to date. Also, the people showed no enthusiasm for such a campaign. Troops returning home from Louisburg had talked freely of the hardships and horrors of war, and military life had lost much of its appeal.

But the most important of the factors deterring an attack on Quebec was the absence of Indian raids on the colonies' wilderness settlements. If the French left them in peace, the Americans had no desire to carry on the war.

With thoughts of home predominant in the minds of everyone from Sir William Pepperrell to the lowliest private in the ranks, there was general rejoicing at Louisburg, late in May, when a huge flotilla that had crossed the Atlantic from England appeared, Union Jacks fluttering from the mastheads of ships of the line, frigates, and scores of troop transports.

Five regiments of Redcoat infantry had been sent to replace the colonial militiamen. No troops cheered the new arrivals more loudly than the heretofore irreplaceable Rhode Islanders, who were jubilant when they learned that a strong artillery detachment of British Regulars had accompanied the expedition. Major General Harrison F. Wilmot, a veteran of more than twenty-five years' service in the Royal Army, replaced Pepperrell; a retired navy officer, Charles Knowles, had been appointed Governor of Louisburg by the Crown; and the supreme command went to Vice Admiral Lord Townsend, who succeeded Sir Peter Warren.

The conquerors of Louisburg had fulfilled their obligations and were free to return home. Warren, Waldo, and Pepperrell gave each other farewell dinners attended by all of the officers they had commanded, and the departing militiamen and sailors held their own celebrations. The festivities lasted for the better part of a week, and the newcomers from England took over sentry duties and other chores.

The Rhode Islanders enjoyed one final triumph. They challenged their successors to a contest in artillery marksmanship, which they won with ease. Two merchant ships no longer fit for use at sea were used as targets; the Americans sank theirs in less than a quarter of an hour, but the Redcoat gunners were still firing salvos at their brig after the better part of an hour.

After the exhibition, on which the officers had wagered, Pepperrell could not refrain from making a parting jibe. "Your men," he told Lord Townsend, "must look to their laurels and improve their skills. They replace true veterans." British and American newspapers alike gleefully reprinted his remark.

The only Americans who remained at Louisburg were the members of the two regiments that had been the last to arrive. They would stay on seven months longer before being relieved by another contingent from England.

The final ceremonies were held on June 9. The following day, General Pepperrell and the militiamen set out for Boston, escorted by the warships from Massachusetts Bay and Connecticut. Admiral Warren and his squadron left on the same tide, and sailed to England. One of the most extraordinary campaigns in military history had come to an end.

The official closing of the campaign called attention to Louisburg once more, and the entire English-speaking world heaped lavish praise on the men who had taken the fort. In London, speakers in the House of Commons devoted several days to making glowing speeches of tribute. Legislators in each of the American colonial capitals did the same. Public-spirited citizens in Boston proposed that a memorial statue be erected somewhere in the Citadel to commemorate the victory, and men in the other colonies began to send in their contributions.

But General Pepperrell was too sensible a man to permit the erection of statues when some of his veterans were finding it difficult to adjust to civilian life at home. He proposed that, instead, a collection be made to provide every militiaman who had stormed Louisburg with a cash purse. He himself contributed one thousand pounds for the purpose, and Thomas Hancock gave two thousand. A substantial sum was raised over a two-year period, and each veteran was given a bonus of fifty pounds. This sum, although much smaller than the prize money awarded the sailors, was large enough to finance a new start in life for many veterans.

At the time, the most important consequence of the campaign seemed to be the fact that Americans had won an important victory with only token help from Great Britain. But the real significance of the capture of Louisburg did not emerge for another thirty-four years.

Benjamin Franklin, the great statesman, philosopher, author, and scientist, one of the principal architects of American independence, may have been the first to see the true meaning of the campaign of 1745. In 1778, when the infant United States was waging her war for freedom, Franklin was the new nation's special minister to France, and was trying to win French support for the American cause.

In a letter addressed to King Louis XVI, but actually intended for the people of France, Franklin summed up the importance of what had happened more than three decades earlier. "France," he wrote, "inadvertently contributed to the sense of unity our people now enjoy. When troops from many colonies went off together to Cape Breton Island, it was the first time most had traveled beyond the boundaries of their own colonies, the first they had ever seen of other Americans from other places. New Englanders, New Yorkers, Pennsylvanians, and Virginians realized they were not alien to one another, but enjoyed common aspirations, common dreams, and a common love of liberty. Louisburg was the cauldron that melded them into one people.

"The United States of America was born at Louisburg."

15

Governor Charles Knowles, who became the commandant of Louisburg late in the spring of 1746, was not impressed by the strategic or tactical importance of the fortress. "This place," he wrote to King George's ministers in London, "is not worth the effort it would take to defend her. Not only is the climate damp, with incessant fog making existence unbearable, but the fortifications themselves were badly designed and poorly executed. The efforts made by my predecessors to restore her to a good defense posture are completed only in part. In order to do what is necessary to ward off a successful invasion by the foe, I estimate that several thousand laborers would need to work for at least three to four years. The total cost of such preparations would, in my opinion, exceed two hundred and fifty thousand pounds in sterling."

The British government had no intention of paying such a vast sum. Knowles, convinced that Louisburg was not worth keeping, stopped the repair work that General Pepperrell had initiated, and the fort began to deteriorate.

But the French felt otherwise. Louisburg was not only a great bastion, but a symbol of national pride. Acting on direct orders from King Louis XV, the Duc d'Anville, High Admiral of the French navy, began to collect a new fleet—the greatest ever assembled by his nation. More than one hundred and fifty warships gathered at the naval station in Brest during the summer of 1746. France intended to recapture Louisburg, no matter how great the cost, and Governor Knowles' indifference made it appear likely that the effort would succeed.

But once again nature spoiled D'Anville's plans. When the powerful armada put into the port of Rochelle, an auxiliary naval base located in the Bay of Biscay, to pick up final supplies and armaments, a summer gale, the worst experienced along the coast of France for a generation, blew up suddenly. The fleet was caught unprepared. Bolts of lightning started fires on two ships, and the flames quickly spread to others in the closely packed harbor. Mammoth waves caused other vessels to capsize.

D'Anville decided to ride out the storm at sea, and led the ships still afloat out into open waters. But the gale doubled back, still more vessels were sunk, and the rest were scattered. The damage was so extensive that eight ships of the line were rendered unseaworthy.

Still D'Anville was reluctant to abandon his enterprise, and sailed for the New World with a reduced fleet consisting of only four major warships and several smaller vessels. Five other ships of the line were expected to meet him off the coast of Nova Scotia, but failed to appear. The despairing D'Anville retired to his cabin and shot himself. The following day his ships limped back across the Atlantic to France, and attempts to recapture Louisburg were abandoned.

Europe had been exhausted by the long war, and representatives of the major nations met at Aix-la-Chapelle in 1747 to negotiate terms of peace. Technically, at least, Great Britain had defeated France, and Louis XV was forced to relinquish not only Dutch and Belgian towns he had won, but also several valuable enclaves in India. On one point, however, the French monarch was adamant. He demanded the return of Louisburg to France, and his representatives, who were not bluffing, said he would fight again rather than be denied the New World symbol of his glory.

King George and his ministers had no desire to resume the costly war. Treasury funds were low, the weary people were heartily sick of the struggle, and young men were resisting inducements to enlist in the armed forces. The concession of the Indian city of Madras to Great Britain would earn London merchants enormous sums in the cotton trade, and a new era of prosperity was at hand.

The loss of a remote fortress three thousand miles from the British Isles seemed a small price to pay for peace. Undoubtedly the Crown was influenced, too, by Governor Knowles' low opinion of Louisburg's value. And, although the British press had trumpeted the victory of Pepperrell and Warren, most people in Great Britain knew little and cared less about the fate of a far-distant fortress.

So, when the peace treaty was signed in 1748, Louisburg was returned to France.

The people of Britain were surprised, and the Americans were shocked, then furious. There was talk in Boston, Philadelphia, and several smaller communities of asking Sir William Pepperrell to lead his veterans back to Cape Breton Island, defying both Britain and France and holding Louisburg against all comers. The idea was so radical that nothing came of it.

The overall effect of the unexpected cession cost the British dearly. Thousands of Americans, particularly the Louisburg veterans and their families, never again trusted the Crown or its ministers. "We became skeptics," Franklin wrote in 1779, "and who could blame us?"

The transfer of the great fort from the British to the French was accomplished in the summer of 1749. Banquets and fetes were held for ten days, and the troops of both nations paraded. Sir William Pepperrell, who had been invited to attend the ceremonies, curtly declined. The Crown knew better than to invite Sir Peter Warren, who was so enraged that he had been threatening to resign from the Royal Navy.

The French at once began extensive repairs on the Island Battery, the new fort on the cliff that the Americans had started to erect, and the Citadel itself. No money was spared on the efforts, and when the troops who comprised the garrison were unable to complete the task to the satisfaction of engineers from Paris and Quebec, bounties were offered to laborers from New France who would spend one year at Cape Breton Island.

High-ranking French officials were determined to make the fort stronger than ever. New ramparts were added, scores of guns were carried across the ocean from French arsenals, and emplaced in new positions, and the stocks of provisions, gunpowder, and ammunition purchased were so enormous that new cellars had to be scooped out of the earth beneath the Citadel.

In spite of these preparations, however, Louisburg was weaker than ever in her history. Her three governors, who succeeded one another after brief terms of office in the next few years, were far more interested in the gay social life of peacetime than in maintaining the discipline necessary for the protection of a military post. While hired laborers worked on the fortifications, dug new storage cellars, and emplaced new guns, the French troops at Louisburg were idle. Men slept, drank, gambled, and lazed away their days. Neither physically nor emotionally were they prepared to fight.

Apparently the governors of Louisburg failed to recognize the obvious indications that England and France would soon be at war again. The French hold on her New World possessions had been weakened, and Britain coveted them. Frederick the Great, England's close ally, had not yet settled his score with the Austrians, who, in turn, were anxious to recover their national pride at his expense. Other nations, equally restless, were nursing grievances against one another, too. Europe was still a tinderbox.

The new conflict began in 1756, a scant eight
after the Treaty of Aix-la-Chapelle had been signed. In
the New World, where the struggle became known as the
French and Indian War, the Ottawa, Micmac, and Algonkin resumed their raids on the frontier settlements of
England's American colonies. History was repeating itself,
and a new reign of terror began.

For a year England floundered, and in the New World
the French, seizing the initiative, captured a number of
key border posts. Then, in 1757, William Pitt, who had
served a previous term as England's Prime Minister, returned to office. Like Governor William Shirley before
him, Pitt realized that Louisburg was the key to ultimate
victory in North America. Bitterly regretting the generosity
of the British negotiators who had returned Cape Breton
Island to France, he made plans to duplicate the feat of
General Pepperrell and Admiral Warren, and recapture
the great fort.

He needed time to prepare an expeditionary force, so his
first step was to establish a naval blockade that would
prevent the enemy from reinforcing the Louisburg garrison. Sheer chance dealt him a crippling blow when a storm
forced the Royal Navy ships forming a cordon around
Cape Breton Island to disperse for a few days. Before the
fleet could take up its stations again, a convoy of nineteen
French warships and merchantmen slipped into the Louisburg harbor. They were the only French vessels that
managed to reinforce the garrison, the blockade thereafter
becoming airtight. But the damage had been done, and
the task awaiting Pitt's fighting men was made infinitely
more difficult.

Governor Augustin de Drucour of Louisburg, who had
held his post since 1754, should have been prepared for
any emergency. Certainly his long record of service in the
French government indicated that he was an able administrator. But he had been careless, even indifferent,

prior to the outbreak of hostilities, and the morale of his three thousand professional troops was low.

Governor de Drucour swiftly made amends. Discipline was tightened, and troops were given bonuses that helped raise their spirits. The town of Louisburg had grown appreciably in nine years, and all able-bodied men in the community of four thousand were called to service as militia. An appeal made to the Micmac brought eight hundred Indian warriors to the fort.

The warships that had sneaked through the temporarily disrupted lines of the British blockaders vastly increased the French naval strength at Louisburg. Five ships of the line and five frigates were anchored in the harbor, along with a number of smaller vessels. In all, there were more than three thousand sailors in the fleet, which could put about five hundred and fifty cannon into action.

The land batteries, too, were far more powerful than they had been in 1745. Governor de Drucour's domain was protected by two hundred and thirty-six guns, ranging in size from twenty-four-pounders to small howitzers. Heavy guard details were established at all shore points at which Pepperrell's men had landed. The new Island Battery was stronger than the rock that the Rhode Islanders had blasted to bits, and the French believed themselves secure.

Pitt and Lord Jeffrey Amherst, the man he selected as his supreme commander, disagreed. Both men were cautious and imaginative strategists who believed in dealing massive, decisive blows. Their long-range plan was, basically, a simple one. Admiral Edward Boscawen, who was already blockading Louisburg, was ordered to permit no help to reach the garrison. No matter how high the cost in men or ships, Governor de Drucour was to be totally isolated from the outside world until the largest and most powerful expeditionary force ever assembled for duty in the New World swept him into permanent oblivion.

Amherst would lead a great army and navy against Louisburg, hoping to reduce the fortress as rapidly as possible. Then, when the essential gateway to New France had been made secure, he planned to attack Quebec itself. The British goal was nothing less than the acquisition of all Canada, which, once secured, would be kept under British control. Pitt had no intention of repeating the errors of 1748.

In late February, 1758, Lord Jeffrey Amherst sailed from England in an armada consisting of more than two hundred vessels. His naval strength was staggering. He could rely on the support of twenty-three ships of the line, most of them mounting seventy-four guns, and of seventeen frigates. Crowded onto transports were eleven thousand Redcoats, including some of England's finest regiments.

In mid-May, the ships reached the town of Halifax, Nova Scotia, which Amherst used as his invasion headquarters. There he was joined by three thousand more troops. The great majority of them were British Regulars who had been stationed in the colonies, but there was one regiment of American volunteers, commanded by Colonel Gorham, who had served with such distinction in 1745 as the head of Pepperrell's scouts.

Most of the men who seved under Gorham were veterans of the previous Louisburg expedition, who had volunteered to make another assault on the fortress. The Crown had not raised units of American militia for the new attack, however. Amherst thought in professional terms, and neither wanted nor expected he would need the assistance of amateurs. Rarely had any general felt greater self-confidence.

Amherst had good reason to believe he would succeed. His artillery detachments carried one hundred and ten cannon of various sizes; his ammunition included approximately fifty thousand "roundshot," or iron balls, and fifty thousand shells that would explode when they struck their targets. In the holds of his ships were five thousand barrels of gunpowder.

The conscientious Amherst recognized the importance of troop morale, and realized that nothing was of greater significance to soldiers than the care given the sick and wounded. His armada included five hospital ships, all of them fully staffed with physicians and attendants. His medical stores were prodigious, and one of the physicians said that "we have enough bandages to swathe every member of the expedition from head to foot."

Amherst was a man who left nothing to chance. Two members of his staff were students of the new and very uncertain art of weather prophecy. They informed him, separately, that there would be little rain during the first week of June, and that the seas, barring unseasonable winds, would be calm. So, on the afternoon of June 1, 1758, the commander in chief led his forces out of Halifax for the short voyage to Louisburg.

It was far more difficult for the British Regulars to land troops on Cape Breton Island than it had been for Pepperrell's American militiamen. On the third attempt they succeeded, however, and the credit rightfully went to Brigadier James Wolfe. A man of great skill and courage, Wolfe was only thirty-one years old at the time, and before the British campaign in the New World ended, he lost his life and won himself immortality.

The French, heavily outnumbered, were compelled to withdraw from some of their outposts, and De Drucour made the grave mistake of evacuating the fort built on the cliff above the entrance to the inner harbor. This proved his undoing. Wolfe stormed the heights with fifteen hundred men, braving heavy enemy artillery fire, and occupied the position.

That gave the British a base for their artillery, and Amherst pressed his advantage to the full, crowding guns onto the cliff and bombarding both the Island Battery and the Citadel beyond. Meanwhile Admiral Boscawen repeatedly challenged the ships of the inferior French fleet. Whenever a French ship accepted, unable to stand his impudence any longer, he destroyed it.

Boscawen's blockade was not airtight, however. In one of the most dramatic incidents of the campaign, a French ship of the line, the *Aréthuse*, managed to escape, and although somewhat battered, sailed off to France to inform higher authorities of Louisburg's plight. Amherst felt it was necessary to capture the fortress before help could be sent to the garrison from France.

Artillery played a major role in the duel, as it had in Pepperrell's campaign, and Amherst's gunners, like the Rhode Island cannoneers, improved with practice. However, there was a difference in their methods. The Americans had been ingenious; the Redcoats were methodical. Concentrating their fire on individual French guns, Amherst's men destroyed them one by one.

Again and again Amherst found himself employing the tactics used in the previous campaign. He managed, with great difficulty, to gain a foothold on the plain south of the Citadel. A student of Pepperrell's journal, he carried raftlike devices to support his cannon on the swampy ground, and when they were in position he stepped up the pace of his bombardment, putting pressure on Louisburg from two sides.

There was one major difference in the two campaigns. Pepperrell had been careful not to damage the little city of Louisburg. But Amherst was in a hurry, anxious to win a victory before the defenders could be reinforced. So he began to shell the town, and soon after the residents had fled into the Citadel, fires swept through the community, destroying most of the homes and shops.

Wolfe, who had been assigned the unenviable task of reducing the Island Battery, kept his gunners working night and day. The unhappy French, seeing history repeat itself, discovered that the defenders of the Island Battery needed relief every few days. "Men go mad when subjected to a prolonged bombardment," Governor de Drucour wrote.

By July 25, the French had been battered into a state of helpless stupor, and Governor de Drucour raised the white flag of surrender. The second invasion of Louisburg ended in victory, as had the first. British losses were relatively light, the attackers suffering approximately five hundred casualties in killed and wounded, while the French lost almost four and one half times that number.

Lord Jeffrey Amherst returned to England, and Wolfe, in command of that portion of the British army remaining in the New World, went on to Quebec, which he besieged. Both he and Louis Joseph, Marquis de Montcalm, the French commander, were killed in a vicious engagement on the Plains of Abraham before the capital of New France. But Wolfe's tactics carried the field, and France was forced to surrender her entire North American colony to Great Britain.

William Pitt and Amherst discussed Louisburg at length, and in 1760 reached a joint decision of lasting significance. The two serious French defeats on Cape Breton Island afforded a sobering example, and both men realized that England, too, might falter. By order of the Crown, Amherst, as commander in chief of His Majesty's forces in North America, was directed to demolish the fortress of Louisburg, "effectually and entirely."

The order was carried out, to the letter, that same year. By the time the Royal Army and Navy had finished, literally nothing remained of the great Citadel's walls and ramparts, towers and platforms. Peace descended on Cape Breton Island, a peace that has remained unbroken for more than two hundred years.

Memorials were erected to the gallant members of both expeditions that captured the great bastion, and another honors the equally courageous French defenders. But it remained for John Hancock, President of the Continental Congress in the American Revolution, to provide the most effective statement of the campaign's significance.

"Louisburg has become a wild and desolate place," he said in an address to his fellow citizens of Massachusetts. "But the rumble of cannon will forever echo there, for it was there that Americans first learned to stand shoulder to shoulder in the cause of liberty. We, and the generations who will come after us, will for all time be indebted to those brave men, a glorious and fantastic breed."

PRINCIPAL BIBLIOGRAPHY

Almon, Albert, *Louisburg, the Dream City of America,* Glace Bay, Nova Scotia, 1934.

Baker, Henry M., *The First Siege of Louisburg, 1745,* The Rumford Press, Concord, N.H., 1909.

Bradstreet, Dudley, *Diary During the Siege of Louisburg,* John Wilson & Son, Cambridge, Mass., 1897.

Drake, Samuel A., *The Taking of Louisburg, 1745,* Lee & Shepard, Boston, 1890.

Hamilton, Edward P., *The French and Indian Wars,* Doubleday & Co., New York, 1962.

Huidekoper, F. L., *The Sieges of Louisburg,* Society of Colonial Wars, Washington, 1914.

Louisburg Journals, Louis E. de Forest, ed., Society of Colonial Wars, Washington, 1932.

McLennan, J. S., *Louisburg from Its Foundation to Its Fall,* Macmillan & Co., London, 1913.

Pepperrell, Sir William, *Journals,* American Antiquarian Society, Worcester, Mass., 1910.

Roberts, W. W., *The First Siege of Louisburg, Told in the Words of Its Captors,* John Wilson & Son, Cambridge, Mass., 1889.

Runk, L. B., *Fort Louisburg*, Pennsylvania Society of Colonial Wars, Philadelphia, 1911.

Wood, William, *The Great Fortress*, Glasgow, Brook & Co., Toronto, 1915.

INDEX